The Late-Blooming Flower
and Other Poems

Linda Love

visual poetry by photographers
Janine Cooper Ayres • csgee • Donald H. Gudehus • D.V. Hardy
JCMDI Digital Imaging • Miranda Knowles • Kamy Merithew
Bill Norton • Frank M. Toothaker
and artists
Nancy Fierro • Diane Shields • Michael Vernetti

Other books by Linda Love

The Cow Who Said Quack

ISBN 9780578350127
© 2022 Linda Love
All rights reserved.

Graphic design and typesetting by Wayne Kehoe.
waynekehoe.com

Cover Photo by Donald H. Gudehus.
parfaitimage.com

Biography of Linda Love

I have always loved poetry, from the time I was very small, when my mother read children's verses to me. The lilting sound of her voice, the rhythmic rhymes, the delight of the words, were magic to me.

Since that time, I have enjoyed reading poetry, as well as writing some poems and short children's stories. But it was to music that I became the most devoted. Music was in the family. My mother was a piano teacher, my father a singer. So I became a concert pianist and have shared the beauty of music with many audiences. In the past few years, a condition called focal dystonia has limited my ability to play any technically difficult piece of music. This caused a severe year-long depression. But fortunately, I discovered that there is still much wonderful music I can play, and by listening to my body, have become my own physical therapist.

Recent years have seen a great outburst of poetry, hence one might say I am a late-blooming flower. But for me, writing has nothing to do with time, late or early. Poems simply ask to be written, and I gladly oblige. Some are written in a flash, others require more working out, exchanging one word or phrase for another, or varying the rhythm, until the form is in accordance with my vision. My inspiration comes from Nature, people, events, and the circumstances of daily life. Most of the poems in this book were written between 2014 and 2022. Some earlier poems are identified by date.

For me, music and poetry are tributaries of one stream. As rhythm is the heartbeat of music, so it is in poetry. Each poem, each piece of music, has its own rhythm, which is inextricably tied to its meaning. One's imagination can soar over the rhythm, but not without it. Music is poetry in sound, poetry is music in words. Both use imagination to clothe feelings which are universal to all human beings. We "understand" music and poetry because we are a part of it.

I once had a piano teacher who said, "The world of imagination is as real as any other world." And so I invite you to wander through the pages of this book, led by your imagination and your heart into that inexplicable soul we share together.

The photography in this book features scenes from Nature. Also included are two paintings and a mosaic.

Is not Nature the supreme artist, and the ever-changing colors, shapes, scents, textures, tastes, and sounds of each day poetry? When we are fully present, without the imposition of our values, prejudices, comparisons, and measurements, are we not an indivisible part of Nature? And so it is in this book, that the poetry and the pictures are inextricably intertwined, related to each other like two branches of the same tree.

With much appreciation to the photographers and artists who so generously contributed their visual poetry to this book.

Dedicated to my mother, Sylvia Amsterdam Shlutz (1911 – 2006)
Who read poems to the child in a far-away time that was me.

Reaching

Alone but not lonely
I face the challenge
Of the diminishing moments
Inner peace embraces my spirit
I caress the lives of those I trust
My quiet self soars upward
This day I sing!
Life is full of melody
If we but listen to the meaningful sounds and
Feel the harmonious elegy of Nature

Sylvia Amsterdam Shlutz

*Words have flavors
That ask to be savored*

Linda Love

Table of Contents

Nature

17	A late-blooming flower
19	Dawn awakens quietly
21	Intellect has a furrowed face
23	A Paean to Coyotes
25	The wind staggered as a drunkard all night
27	My house is prim and proper
29	Startled, as I spied them
31	Uncoiling
33	Have you ever seen
35	Downtown
37	To A Young Hawk
39	The snail in his shell
41	An Invitation
45	An Encounter
49	An Unwelcome Visitor
53	Wanderings
59	A Surprising Discourse
63	Rooms
67	I lie awake, waiting for him
69	Summer 2021
75	Moments
81	I found a treasure on the forest floor
83	Unanswered Question
87	Twilight
89	Two Impressions 1988
91	A butterfly is a poem
93	A Paean to Spring

Love

- **97** Little boat rocking on a stormy sea
- **99** A Picnic Table
- **101** One night I stumbled in the dark
- **103** A Place of Honor
- **107** Ketubah
- **111** A Song of Passages
- **113** An Old Romance
- **117** That fish over there!
- **119** I'm Just Me
- **123** Nuances on Long-distance Friendship
- **127** Unanswered
- **129** Ambling down a country lane one day
- **133** Friendship
- **135** A Song of Solace
- **137** You are only a memory now
- **139** When you see
- **143** Birthday Greeting
- **147** I didn't see her as she approached me
- **151** The Garden

Society

155	Peace
157	Achievement is a tawdry thing
159	A Litany
161	A Curious Story
163	Rap
165	Fame is so very slight a whim
167	pews compress so narrow a space
169	A house has many corners
171	A Whimsical Tale
177	The Fabrication
181	Two November Poems
183	An Oration
187	People of many talents
189	A Math Lesson
193	A Search
199	A Narrative
203	A Cautionary Tale
207	Nuances on New Year's Day
211	Turning Point
213	Folksong – A Veteran's Tale
215	Abstractions are daunting
217	A Note on Devices
223	Evolution
225	Refrain
231	Adjournment
237	Masked in medieval armor
239	A Wish
245	An Inquiry

Life and Death

253 Ideals are virtues
255 If
257 Disowned
259 In Search of a Prayer
261 Goliath Versus David
265 Epitaph
267 from an inscription
269 Immortality is a word
271 Leavetaking
273 I had a vision of my life
275 A Snapshot
281 Shopping
285 Sickness is a garment
287 Requiem
289 Suffering is deemed a virtue
291 Variations on a Theme
301 Nuances on Loneliness
305 Convalescence – A Prelude
309 Funny thing about stains
313 There is something so disquieting
315 Brief
317 Immortality stands ready
319 The longest journey there must be
321 Drawn to eccentricity
323 What can I say to you, dear friend
325 Time embezzles Memory
327 Do you have a secret drawer
329 Faith
331 The Masters are oft quoted
333 Someone's been sowing a secret
335 Obituary
337 "What is Life?"
339 I am the river
343 Translation

346 Index of Photography

Nature

A late-blooming flower
does not know it is late;
blooming without knowing,
it does not hesitate

Requiring no company
it stands alone;
conspicuous with color,
all celebrate

Dawn awakens quietly
as a kitten on velvet paws,
and sweeping the dusty stars away,
puts on her pinkest shawl.

She closes the door of Sister Night,
giving her sleep its sway,
and places a log upon the hearth
to warm the house all day.

Arraying herself in a light blue gown,
she arranges her tresses of clouds,
then donning jewels of sparkling dew,
colors all the town.

How quaint this little lady is,
who goes about her task,
never once complaining,
never once asked.

The Late-Blooming Flower *and Other Poems*

Intellect has a furrowed face,
A tillage of straight lines,
Plowed with great profundity
By its grasp throughout Time.

But I would rather be the truant,
disorderly, unruly,
in my unwrinkled flight
be elusive as a Monarch
swirling through the air
in exuberant orange raiment,
content to alight on flowers for afternoon tea,
sipping their sweet nectar for
just a moment or two –

        then bidding each one adieu.

For my dear friend Donald Gudehus, whose exquisite photography of butterflies allows us a window into their world of beauty.

The Late-Blooming Flower *and Other Poems*

A Paean to Coyotes

In a cocoon of blankets laying
on a still and moonless night,
suddenly an explosion of cries wild and bloodthirsty
punctuate the skies

I find it strangely soothing,
this fierce lullaby,
and as it preys upon my ears,
I ask myself why?

I think it is the honesty,
undisguised by masks,
a directness of intention,
a laying out of facts

The sobriety of survival,
that and only that,
unblanketed by euphemisms
and the chicanery of traps

Neither spoiled by a note of impropriety,
prowling the hills in packs for game,
nor an accent bowed of the head in shame,
for the pact that Nature has ordained

The Late-Blooming Flower *and Other Poems*

The wind staggered as a drunkard all night,
howling through the town;
birds cowered in their nests, unable to rest,
the houses shook in fright.

He chased the leaves right down the street,
as if admonishing his brood,
and with a heavy handshake greeted branches,
which promptly split in two.

Dancing with the moonlit shadows,
he weaves around and about,
in ruffian manner and ragged dress,
how flaunts this uninvited guest!

Until reeling and cavorting, he can stand no more,
in inebriated stupor tumbles to the floor;
just then, as gentle dawn arrives,
a hummingbird, poised, hovers in the skies.

My house is prim and proper,
Of orderly bent,
The substance of a fugue
Reveals her content.

But outside in the garden
Breathes a realm unbridled, free,
Airs of efflorescence
Unrestrained by regularity.

How whimsical, how charming,
That one nature could contain
This yin and yang that coexist
In such quixotic bliss!

The Late-Blooming Flower *and Other Poems*

Startled, as I spied them,
were fields of fallen stars,
constellations clustered,
descended from afar.

They sang in rapturous wonder,
waving carefree in the breeze,
a chorus of countless colors,
united in harmony.

They much preferred the earth, confided,
to cold firmament above;
not once complaining their time was brief,
flowered together in peace.

*after a walk amongst spring wildflowers
in the hills behind Elizabeth Lake, California*

The Late-Blooming Flower *and Other Poems*

Uncoiling,
he vanished quickly,
as a year
departing will,
disappeared in
the brush,
bequeathing
on the dust
of memory's sill
but a trace

(for a snake)

Have you ever seen
A stream meandering
As angles in a square,
Or tides at a seashore
In lines straight and fair?

Calculations are convenient,
Convention secure,
But Nature employs no disguises
To pretend that she endures.

The Late-Blooming Flower *and Other Poems*

Downtown

How tall the buildings tower!
How diminutive are we!
That selfsame hands would fashion such disparity,
What a bewildering geometry!

To A Young Hawk

Aristocratic, he perched there,
Not a leaf was on the tree,
It seemed that he did so
Just to keep it company.

I watched him from a window,
I ventured not outside,
For fear that I might startle him
And flight would take to hide.

Enrobed in princely raiments,
Feathers downy-soft and grey,
To the ashen hue of his
Barkened castle he blended perfectly.

From side to side he turned his head,
Animated by design,
Scanning doubtless for an unsuspecting prey
To swoop upon his claws to lay.

I know not how many minutes passed,
One dares not count the time
In the presence of such royalty
Sporting golden eye divine.

Then deigning to turn his back on me, he flew off,
Vanishing in answer to some unknown call.
Though time has flown over a year since then,
The spell has not been broken at all.

The snail in his shell
Is comfortable, just so;
The brink of his economy
Is all he needs to know.

An Invitation

Air is no outsider.
Admitted freely,
it goes about everywhere,
shunning no-one

No doors are closed to it,
no windows barred.
Holding court equally with paupers and kings,
earthworms it honors,
birds it helps sing.

Knowing no boundaries,
it abounds;
Needing no passport,
it surrounds

Encroaching on no-one,
it fills every space;
Abiding without fear,
it cooperates

Isms divide and multiply
in furious appeal,
seeking to unite,
but ever engaged in fight.

Pervasive, not invasive,
air in true balance shares,
provisions given abundantly
so that no cupboard lies bare

Friend of friends and foes alike,
(humble giver of Life),
why can't we learn
from you no strife?

Filling every crevice
with your unerring rhythm,
why can't we learn from you
to obliterate schism?

The Late-Blooming Flower *and Other Poems*

An Encounter

Do I dare?

Approach the little fellow
With violet-blue wings,
Sipping sweet nectar
From a blue-violet flower
On a rosemary bush
In my garden?

Do I dare?

Disturb his amorous encounter,
His rapturous clasp,
With soundless feline steps
Taken with bated breath?

He does appear undaunted
By my presence . . . .

Irresistibly drawn by
A mysterious force,
One small step
Follows another.

I am right beside him.

Will he, in a flash,
Flitter away,
Alarmed by a bypasser
Who dares disrupt his tryst?

Still he stays, monogamist,
True to his pursuit,
Refusing to be wooed.

Do I dare
Attempt the impossible?
Reach out and tremulously touch
His folded gossamer wings?

Still, still he rests,
Fearlessly faithful to his flower,
United with her in Nature's bower,
Moored to his kiss
Drunk with lovers' bliss,
Receiving me with sympathy
Innocent of antipathy.

I'd like to think
He reveled in my nearness,
Dissimilar to his peers,
Who overcome with trepidation,
Would not lose an instant
To gaily flutter away.

But he, he dared to share,
This brave little fellow,
And though time has taken wing,
I am indelibly wedded
To the space
Where we were bonded
In a magical embrace.

*Dedicated to my dear friend Donald Gudehus,
whose beautiful photographs of butterflies
touch our lives.*

The Late-Blooming Flower *and Other Poems*

An Unwelcome Visitor

There's one thing
About the wind.
You can't argue with it.

It's in your face,
Full-fisted,
And won't back down.

No matter what you say,
It always gets its way.
Whatever line you take,
It never admits a mistake.

Dominating the conversation,
It has the last word.
Can you sneak your view in edgewise?
Don't even try,

Or attempt to find a crack
In its argument
Bent to a self-righteous will.

Can you take a detour,
Or gracefully bow out?
No, it won't allow it,
Even if you shout.

Standing in your way,
It holds its ground,
Blocks you at every twist and turn,
Keeping you at bay.

And as if that isn't enough,
It pushes this, shoves that,
Discourteously out of the way,
Having no thought whatsoever
To sowing disarray.

Unable to resist the temptation,
Trees imbibe great draughts,
Swaying like drunken men,
Reeling and weaving about.

Leaves chase each other
Down the street,
Like children playing tag,
Never for a moment allowed to rest,
Not permitted to lag.

As if Winter had fallen
Head over heels for Spring,
Courting her at every chance,
Seeds white as snowflakes
Swirl madly through the air,
Impelled to the ground
In a frenzied dance.

Shamelessly spreading gossip,
Waves of grasses chatter away,
Bringing glee to some,
But to others dismay.

Even rocks are shaken
From their fold,
Rolling in choruses
Loosed from gravity's hold.

Relentlessly whistling at high pitch,
The gusts snuff every sound out.
Above the din,
Nothing can be heard,
Not the song of a bird,
Or insects on the wing.

No constable dares arrest the scoundrel
For disturbing the peace.
Inevitably it escapes without warning
The moment he sternly cries "Cease"!

Then just as you think
Your visitor will never depart,
The maelstrom collapses,
Like an arrow in flight
That halts its trajectory
Before it alights,
Leaving in its wake
A tumultuous mess.

Some would label it destruction.
Others would call it creation.

Reader, what is your guess?

The Late-Blooming Flower *and Other Poems*

Wanderings

Funny,
How you can walk
By something
Every day
And not notice
Anything peculiar about it
Until one day in one breath
You do
And everything about it
Changes.
Funny, too,
How you can put on
A figure of speech
Like an old piece of clothing
Hung in a closet
And wear it out
Until it bursts
At the seams
Because you hold it dear
And have a penchant
For stretching your budget.

Take, for example,
My neighborhood,
A small patchwork of houses
Quilted together,
Cupped like a rookery
Nestled in between mountains,
Worn by my footsteps
Meandering through the streets
Like a familiar maze.

There it happened,
On a day not too long ago,
When casually passing by
An empty lot,
I did a double-take,
Stopping in my tracks.

Empty lot!
The words screamed at me.
How odd a title for a piece of land!
Empty of what?
When this plot of earth
Is a thriving community
Populated by a medley of
Grasses, shrubs, insects,
Lizards, squirrels, snakes,
Scores of invisible inhabitants,
And birds who drop in
For an occasional visit?

My mind was suddenly arraigned
By a whole catechism of expressions
Parading in costumes
Designed by my fellow
Lords of creation.

Vacant lot,
Undeveloped land,
Unimproved lot,
Land for sale,
All special designations
Assigned to plots of earth
Begging to be appropriated
By their owners,
Or else condescendingly
Protected by them
In a cocoon of open space.

Curious,
How a bent of mind,
Like a tree slanted by the winds,
Circumscribes one's view.

Is it not written
That the lot of mankind
Is to have dominion
Over the earth
And all its creatures?
Does it not follow therefore that land
Has no value in itself,
But is merely
An unkempt wild beast,
Whose destiny is to be lassoed, corralled,
Tamed into submission?

Except
For an afterthought
Of token patches set aside
As a nod to posterity
Because, oddly enough,
Everyone needs a breath of green
Once in a while.

As my mind
Was whittling away
At the deep roots of dogma,
It suddenly did an about-face,
Wandering far away from
The empty lot
Which first held my attention captive.

I found myself
In another neighborhood
Where, once upon a time,
There was a little girl
Who lived on a wide street
Lined with trees whose roots
Threatened to uproot sidewalks,
Bordered by affable houses
Fringed by tidy lawns and pretty flower beds.

I wandered to a place
More than halfway down the block,
To which she was irresistibly drawn,
As if captive to a magic spell.

Almost hidden between two houses,
It was hers to sojourn,
Her special place
Uncircumscribed by geometry,
Where space burst its seams
And time had no destination.

She did not have to
Knock on the door
Or ask permission to enter.
It entranced her in
With choirs of green grasses,
Where buried treasure beckoned
And one enchantment
Yielded to another.

Wandering back to the present,
My mind bent sadly to how,
In the name of dominion,
That special place
Must now be uprooted,
Officially titled lot for sale,

And rudely ousted to make way
For another affable home,
The magic spell broken,
The grasses gone,
Hemmed into a space
Where it fell,
The innocent victim
Of a uniform system.

But my thoughts did not stop there.
Further on they wandered,
To a place deep in the recesses of my mind,
Sheltered from the tentacles
Of human tenacity.

Nestled there
I found that special place,
Free, wild, undisturbed,
As if held in a charm ,
Where a little girl
Could still wander at will.

A hidden plot of land
That was full but empty,
Empty but full.

Protected.

A Surprising Discourse

Isn't it strange that no-one has ever chided
Mother Nature on being such a sloppy housekeeper?
After all, she doesn't tidy up, pick up after herself,
Dust her furniture, sweep the floor,
Or take out the trash.

With no apparent geometry, rhyme or reason,
She nonchalantly clutters her domain
With trifles and trinkets and memorabilia
And what-have-you.
Her extravagance knows no bounds.

Just look at her appearance – how slovenly it is.
She doesn't care to comb her hair or put on make-up.
Impetuously she dyes her tresses
In all sorts of outlandish colors,
Brazenly showing them off.
A patchwork of fabrics sewn together is her dress.
Worn today, discarded tomorrow.
Strewn about her abode lie the
Tattered remnants of her worn-out garments.
No self-respecting woman would ever dare show
Herself in public the way she does.

And yet she is the most admired woman of all time,
Praised for her beauty, stylish dress,
Unsurpassed in graciousness, hospitality,
And the magnificent décor of her palatial home.

Many have sought to imitate her.
Though she deceives no-one,
Doesn't cover anything up,
Or play a game of pretend,
Her beauty is ever elusive.
Though countless suitors have tried,
No-one has succeeded in capturing it.

Shrouding herself in mystery,
She reigns in majestic splendor,
Indecipherable, ever-changing,
Her secret hidden from view.
Her imperfection perfection,
Invoking wonder after wonder.

Is it any wonder that no-one has ever admonished her?

The Late-Blooming Flower *and Other Poems*

Rooms

There is something comforting about monotony, like being on a train and listening to the constant rhythm of the wheels. So it is on a flat trail which never provokes, never challenges, and seems to go on forever with no vanishing point in sight. No gamble here. Just an unruffled security where there are no opposites, no conflicts, where everything is laid out bare of horizons, bewitching and beckoning. The predictability takes one onward and onward, quite dissimilar to the enticement that lures one to go around the proverbial corner to see what lies beyond an immediate view.

This is the monotone of the California Aqueduct, its path hugging the ruler-straight edge of the oddly deep blue water channeled to specification in its concrete bed. An anomaly asserting itself in a light beige desert waving with hills, accented here and there with shades of green that scramble to find water to support their sparse existence. A Matisse landscape of flat brushstrokes, a few colors, a few shapes, clear outlines, diminished of detail. Life simplified, stripped of everything but the bare essentials. Our senses luxuriate in this framework of calm predictability. Even the wind is constant, irrevocable, punctuating the water with ripples bobbing up and down with the sporadic ducks that look strangely out of place here. Eternity was never so well described. Jarring one's sense of complacency are occasional signposts warning unwary walkers to stay clear of the water. Nothing is perfect.

Whenever I hike with my husband, though, I am conditioned to expect the unexpected, as the paradoxical figure of speech goes. I just don't know <u>when</u> this unexpected will occur, <u>when</u> he will suddenly and purposefully wander off trail, unannounced to me. I only know that at some point it is inevitable. I have no choice but to go willingly, or unwillingly tag along, bound to follow him like the biblical Ruth – "Whither thou goest I will go". This is despite the fact that I do not have the slightest inclination in my life to follow anyone.

And so on this straight path on a straight sunny day with everything neatly and predictably in place in the mesmerizing rut of monotony, I was jarred by the realization that Life had thrown me a curve. Literally.

Off he went, down a curving dirt road leading to God only know where. I follow, my fealty pulling me along. Steadily we descend. Suddenly he stops, riveted in place. I too stop, as if obeying a traffic signal. Some trees are ahead of us. "Do you hear what I hear"? he says. My attention must have fled from me. I heard nothing. But moments later, I found myself listening to the clear, melodious sounds of birds, a whole choir of them, coming from the trees, and hidden by the green leaves sparkling in the bright sunlight.

Slowly we approached the trees, and in a twinkling, as if a Pandora's Box had been opened, hundreds of birds were flying about, coming out from the trees and a community of cattails that, upon finding just enough water to survive, had settled there. This just a hair's breadth from the inexorably flowing aqueduct whose water rights had been secured by city dwellers!

Twirling, swirling above us the black birds flashed splashes of red on their wings in a dizzying display – encircling, landing, encircling, landing – all done with the perfectly synchronized grace of a corps de ballet. Many landed on the rungs of a barb-wired fence, looking like black notes on a music staff. We, a privileged audience of two, were privy to an earth-shattering event, never having seen this multitude of congregants in a flock of red-winged blackbirds. We could only gaze in timeless wonder, the monotone of the aqueduct eclipsed from our view.

The curving path led us back to the aqueduct. Time resumed its ticking on the straight edge of Life.

"You never know what you will find", says my adventurer husband. It's his mantra, the same but never the same, spurring him on to detour away from a plainly laid out path, instead taking an unknown tributary. What is uneventful suddenly becomes eventful, taking us out of our predictable existence. We wander together through Nature's art gallery, from a room of Matisse to a room of Van Gogh, from luxuriating in the planned, flat yet vibrant colors planed of detail, only to be derailed by the violently expressive, impulsive, and wild, where the rough-hewed paint seems to leap out of the canvas, like the red-winged blackbirds from the trees.

Life has many rooms contained in one building. Many artists. Many colors. Each stands alone, yet complements the others. Each needs the other to define its existence, its meaning. The straightness of one line, the curving of another, the ordinary nesting within the extraordinary. To be confined in one room is not to see the whole. The syncopated rhythm of one room highlights the strict meter of another. One balances the other. All one must do is take the first step, turning the corner into another room, curving from the known to the unknown. Because "You never know what you will find".

Dedicated to my husband Frank,
with much appreciation for opening new vistas to me

I lie awake, waiting for him,
My ears tuned toward the door,
My eyes assembled to the task
Of greeting him once more.

Eternity escapes right through the gate,
The moon lets out a sigh,
Surely 'twill be soon he'll knock,
As he promised by and by.

My eyes flutter open,
Sunlight is flooding in,
The moon has fled out of dread
For what the morn will bring.

My heart drops down to the floor.
Have I been betrayed once more?

The door's wide open,
He found the key,
He's come and gone
Without notifying me.

How dare he trespass without my ken,
Silently stealing away,
When all I ever asked of him
Is to be a friend and stay.

(Sleep)

Summer 2021

Heat. Heat.
Everywhere heat.
Heat stifling.
Heat sizzling.
Heat suffocating.
Heat smoking.
Heat steaming.
Heat snarling.
Heat screeching.
Heat stealing.
Heat standing.
Heat sitting.
Heat swirling.
Heat swooning.
Heat scooting.
Heat saddling.
Heat sweating.
Heat slithering.
Heat surrounding.
Heat soaring.
Heat sighing.
Heat sapping.
Heat snapping.
Heat slashing.
Heat sawing.
Heat saturating.
Heat scrambling.
Heat scampering.
Heat scattering.
Heat scintillating.
Heat seething.
Heat scolding.
Heat scorching.
Heat scalding.

Heat simmering.
Heat smoldering.
Heat scarifying.
Heat spilling.
Heat stinging.
Heat singeing.
Heat scouring.
Heat scowling.
Heat seizing.
Heat sifting.
Heat shifting.
Heat scuffling.
Heat scurrying.
Heat seeping.
Heat separating.
Heat segregating.
Heat settling.
Heat shackling.
Heat shimmering.
Heat shocking.
Heat shoving.
Heat showering.
Heat shrieking.
Heat shriveling.
Heat sickening.
Heat scrawling.
Heat stupefying.
Heat stultifying.
Heat surging.
Heat squirming.
Heat stammering.
Heat stymieing.
Heat shivering.
Heat snaking.
Heat shaking.
Heat smarting.
Heat sickening.

Heat searing.
Heat shearing.
Heat sulking.
Heat shrinking.
Heat scandalizing.
Heat shooting.
Heat shutting.
Heat shuttering.
Heat scuffling.
Heat shortening.
Heat shoving.
Heat shrouding.
Heat shuddering.
Heat settling.
Heat scalding.
Heat sticking
Heat slobbering.
Heat snaring.
Heat soaking.
Heat softening.
Heat spanning.
Heat spasming.
Heat spewing.
Heat spiking.
Heat spluttering.
Heat stuttering.
Heat stomping.
Heat sprawling.
Heat stalling.
Heat scribbling.
Heat spreading.
Heat spurting.
Heat squandering.
Heat squashing.
Heat stagnating.
Heat staring.
Heat startling.

Heat starving.
Heat slaving.
Heat staying.
Heat stewing.
Heat storming.
Heat striking.
Heat strutting.
Heat subjugating.
Heat sucking.
Heat supplanting.
Heat suppressing.
Heat surging.
Heat sweeping.
Heat swelling.
Heat swooping.
Heat swimming.
Heat swindling.
Heat spoiling.
Heat somnambulating.
Heat simpering.
Heat scampering.
Heat smirching.
Heat scorning.
Heat smothering.
Heat silencing.

Heat. Heat.
Everywhere heat.

Heat. Heat.
Everywhere.

Heat. Heat.

Heat.

The Late-Blooming Flower *and Other Poems*

Moments

rain in the night
children quarreling
disappear into
big Sun

how have you been?
fine.
behind the word the story hides.
let's draw the curtain.

the moon lies still over
the empty night
I look at you,
asleep over there
the moon goes silently by.

orange poppy
punctuating November
I pause

time slips
between my fingers
on its way to the sea

little girl
riding her bicycle in circles
stops to greet me

unable to contain itself
grass laughs its way
to the sun

lingering
on the cheek of Life
sadness

there are
no treatment options
death

shadow passing soundlessly
over the moon
a sliver of light winks at me

your large hand
encloses mine
we nest together

scribbling hieroglyphics
across a blue slate
children vanish

birth
soft downy feathers
tickle the earth

a school of fish
caught in a net of rules
one, blind, struggles to be free
succeeds

welcoming
a breeze
leaves burst into song

three lines
three streams
one river

Time
stepping not backwards
roots

icicles
stones
meet in spring thaw

dark clouds
threaten with rain
crowdburst

liberated
having served their time
leaves

a community of rocks
huddles together for warmth
a frieze of Time

between the lines
of your face
I read history

an itinerant deer
rests on a ledge
Earth warms quietly

waiting for a retiree
a leaf on a park bench

teapot hovering
over my cup
waiting to be filled

seeking light
boughs hug the ground

thirsty
Earth sticks out
her tongue

skyscrapers
framing narrow streets
people pencil paths

walking in your footsteps
suddenly I lose my way

my neighbor's
motion detector
a cat steals by

rapper under
an umbrella
I strain to hear the rain

cherry picker
the checkout cashier
accepts food stamps

The Late-Blooming Flower *and Other Poems*

I found a treasure on the forest floor,
Where gold was mined in days of yore.
A slender feather,
It was blue and gray,
Fallen blithely from the sky
As a blue jay flew by.

I thanked him for it,
And carried it home,
Where it will stay,
No more to roam

Amongst the trees by a forest stream
Where Nature does her feathers preen,
Where blue jays squawk and slyly look
For food to steal from a camper's nook.

I laughed when I saw that one had snatched
An almond on our table cached.
Clever bird! I'll share with you.
You must also have your due.

And I my treasure will forever hold,
A memory of your prank,
Worth more to me than a nugget of gold,
If the truth be told.

The Late-Blooming Flower *and Other Poems*

Unanswered Question

One tree,
Two branches,
One thrives,
The other dies.

A great snow fell
Falling and falling
From an endless
Sky of white.
No end in sight.

Heavy it lay
On the limbs
Of trees.

Great branches fell crashing
To the ground,
Their grieving weight
To snow was bound.

On one day, one day,
Still more snow came.
How could the limbs
Resist the strain

To a tree not tall,
Leaves of plum red
On two branches small,
One succumbed, dead.

Shriveled leaves
That once wore life
Now take on
Tarnished strife

Of broken wings
That cannot fly,
That cannot soar
In sunshine sky.

Sporting festivities
Is the other, untouched.
A parade of flowers
Followed by leaves
Waving red banners
In the breeze.

One can never ask,
One can never answer,
Why one bough was injured
Beyond repair,
While the other
From the selfsame fate
Was spared

On a day
That a great snow
Fell without a lull.

Do not ask.
There is no-one
To tell.

The Late-Blooming Flower *and Other Poems*

Twilight

One evening I saw a duck
Standing at the edge of a pond,
I facing him, his back to me.
Statuesque, mute of movement,
He stood there.
I stood, unmoving, with him.
Perhaps he had winged his journey
To this shore for many years.
It was a home to him.
But now the pond was vanishing.
Soon it would be gone,
Evaporated into the firmament,
Never to return.

One duck.
One pond.

Seeing this,
An infinite sadness
Engulfed me.

The Late-Blooming Flower *and Other Poems*

Two Impressions 1988

New York
It was so strange to walk on the streets, or in the park, and see everybody in their own world, busy, ambitious, avoiding any contact with another. And to see the little sticks of trees on the streets, put there like lollipops to appease a child-like craving for a natural treat. And the noise level was so high, like the tall buildings which dwarf menacingly the starkly vulnerable human beings who walk kissing their feet.

It was unbearably hot today, and now, as if the sky is making peace with the earth, there is the tongue-in-cheek belly roar of thunder, sending rippling laughter breezing through the trees, and the sudden coolness of rain, showering everything with smiles.

A butterfly is a poem
Fleeting through time,
Emerging from its chrysalis
With perfect design.

Gracing the Earth
With a panoply of color,
It seizes the hour
To visit the flowers,
Lingering for a moment
Sipping a cup of sweet tea,
And then without ceremony,
Leaves.

For Anya, who enjoys many an hour of friendship
Over a cup of tea.

The Late-Blooming Flower *and Other Poems*

A Paean to Spring

Spring, dear Spring,
What a charitable lady you are!
You feed the poor,
Clothe the naked,
Shelter the homeless.

Lavishly splashing paint
On your canvas,
You adorn everything
In a bewildering
Array of color,
Fashioning your flowers
With jewel like facets
Dazzling the eye.

With a wave of your wand,
You send a symphony of scents
Wafting through the air.

Birds sing arias
On the stage
Of your grand opera house.

Trees dance
To the tango
Of your breezes.

You never succumb to clichés.

Spring, Spring,
Generous to all,
You leave nothing out.

Who has not
Sung your praises?
Who has not
Gazed with wonder
Upon your gifts,
Given without measure?

Whose heart
Has not been melted
By your welcoming warmth?

Who has not
Been lifted up with hope
By constellations of tiny leaves
Appearing on branches
Which just yesterday
Seemed lifeless?

Who has not
Been blessed by your beauty,
You, who in giving everything,
Become everything?

Love

The Late-Blooming Flower *and Other Poems*

Little boat rocking on a stormy sea,
Don't give up your melody,
But sing as though the world were bright,
Bathed in glowing celestial light

Light that embraces with gentle calm,
Heavenly light that is a balm,
Guiding unseen but sure a course,
Boundlessly immersed in immeasurable source

Source sing song and Source sing light
Obscure the dark unfathomable night;
Safely harbored in stormy sea,
Love, dear Love, envelops me!

A Picnic Table

An umbrella lifted by the wind
fell broke not quite in two,
but something that is mended
is better than brand-new.

The thought of how to make it right,
the turning of the screw,
the nuts, the bolts as fasteners,
the setting of the glue,

Then turning of the thought once more
to set it into place,
the longitude drops snugly down
and verifies its space.

A blustery wind will never guess
that hidden in interim beneath,
a pin is holding firmly
as a sword within a sheath.

Spreading aloft so cheerfully,
green as new-born grass,
my thoughts will ever turn to
the one who made it fast.

For my beloved husband Frank, who made it right.

The Late-Blooming Flower *and Other Poems*

One night I stumbled in the dark
and could not see my way,
the room was spinning like a top
so far was I astray

Straight up you wakened with a start,
and said, "Are you all right?"
as gently placed your hand on mine,
sunlight toppled night

Though now my feet are steady,
rooted as a tree to the spot,
you set my heart aspinning
with love I cannot stop

For my husband Frank

A Place of Honor

When you see a rose
lying on the sidewalk
    pick it up
Hold it between your hands
    gently
Feel it blooming in the warm chalice
    of your flesh
freed from its tomb
    of concrete

Bring it home,
gently a place to honor,
placing as a candle
in the narrow stem
of an earthenware vessel
emblazoned with wildflowers

Do not embalm it
shrouded in the dust laden
cache of decorations
framing your house

Light it on the pyre of your gaze
Let its flaming
destroy your house,
all left of its petals
residing in the melting
    of your heart

Then it will be
    your house
Then it will be
    your heart
the earthen vessel
    of you
no ashes, only love,
    wild flower

Be an alchemist
turning the ordinary
into the extraordinary
    every day

Every day is not
an everyday thing

Ketubah

Let us be married
As the good to the true,
Receive the gift of the moment,
To this we say "I do".

Let us be joined
As the earth to the sky,
The sun to the stars,
The waves to the shore,
The near to the far,
Sharing our love
With all whom we meet.

For love is not an island
Enclosed within itself,
But that intangible light
Uniting us with the whole
Community of life.

We trust love to mold our souls,
Leading us out of the paths
Of comfort, complacency, and habit,
To see the freshness of each other
As in that sparkling silence
After a rain.

We have met each other
In the autumn of our lives,
Aware of the challenges
That life may bring us.

Let not worry, doubt, or fear
Cloud the day,
For love is with us
In every way.

We have faith that
The devotion of our love
Shall hold us steadfast
As an anchor through
Turbulent seas, and
Rejoice in the radiance
Of paths showered with sunshine.

Love is not a promise
To be kept under
Lock and key,
But the daily invitation
Of a living presence.

Today, the beginning
Of our marriage,
Is like the planting of a
Seed in the earth.

We understand that the
Seed needs to be nurtured
With care and attention
In order for it to grow.

It must also be
Protected from harm.
We alone are responsible.
Gladly we take on
This responsibility.

As a symbol of our
New life together,
We plant this seed
And give it water.
We are now in
Each other's care.

Written for the marriage of Frank Toothaker and Linda Love
June 22, 2014
A Ketubah is a marriage covenant
In the Jewish tradition.

The Late-Blooming Flower *and Other Poems*

A Song of Passages

Does the sun think of setting
as it courses to the west?
Or the leaf, in its falling,
harbour any regrets?
The fledgling, when flying,
look back to the nest?
Or rosebush in winter,
fear what comes next?

Then, dearest, if we of elements
like these are made,
let not our passages be marred
by pendulums of clocks,
records and accountings,
and the rising smoke of doubt.

But unwinding the strains
from the spool of our thoughts,
vibrate in orb fundamental with these,
threadbare as the wind,
neither lingering nor straying
from the symmetry of Love,
    single string.

An Old Romance

One day you embarked on a journey to a faraway land. You said you had to work for wages. It has been one year to the day since you left. Today, as always, I will walk to the shore to wait for you. I put on the beautiful sky-blue dress with a pattern of white birds that you once gave me for my birthday. The birds look like they are flying. Oh, how I wish I were a bird and could fly to you, beloved of my heart! I would land on your shoulder and you would put me in a blue and white cage. You would hold me in your hand and I would sing to you.

I open the door into the bright sunshine. My steps are light with hope. My wooden shoes sound like the wild beating of my heart on the cobblestone pavement. On narrow streets like rivulets I walk past the brightly colored houses, some yellow, some blue, some purple, with steeply pitched roofs built to shed the burden of heavy snow when it falls in winter. Each house has a tidy garden with pretty flowers in window boxes, enclosed within a white picket fence. My steps quicken. At last the sea, the sea! I remove my shoes and stumble through the hot sand like an awkward gull. The west wind plays with my skirt as if it were a sail. I reach the shore. My eyes are fixed on the distant horizon, straining to catch a glimpse of you. I call out your name, listening for an echo from far away. But all I see and all I hear are the white seabirds with their piercing cries circling overhead.

The sea is azure, blue as your eyes that seemed to sparkle with sunshine when you looked at me. But now it is high tide, the sea is rough, and the wind is ruffling up the water with swirling white-caps and towering waves that pound the shore. I immerse my feet in the water as it rushes in and out, kissing my feet as it flows and ebbs. Sometimes I venture farther out and have to run quickly from a wave that threatens to engulf me. Delicate little shorebirds run with me, as if we are playing a game of tag with the sea.

I wait patiently, as always, but there is no sign of you. The red sun is sinking slowly beneath the horizon. There is a bright green flash. Then it is gone. With sinking heart, I walk slowly home, never looking back, my head bowed down, as if in prayer. I do not see the colorful houses, nor the gardens. Dusk is turning into night. One by one, stars, like distant candles, illuminate the darkening sky.

I enter my dark house and light some lanterns. Quickly, I eat a simple supper of soup and bread. Before I retire for the night I take a small key and open a drawer in my bureau. Opening a small box inside, I take out a gold ring set with a ruby heart that you had given me as a sign of betrothal. I slip it on my finger and close my eyes for what seems to be an eternity. Tenderly I put it back in the little box. For a moment I look at a faded red rosebud, dried and fragile, that I kept from a bouquet of red roses you once had given me. After locking the drawer, I turn down a light white coverlet on the feather bed, immersing myself in the softness of sleep as if I were tucked safely under the wings of a seabird.

I awaken to a ray of sunshine in my room. Today is filled with fresh hope. I water the flower garden I planted – snapdragons, and pansies that seem to look at me imploringly with their upturned faces. They remind me of something you once said: "You are like a delicate beautiful flower that needs to be watered and cared for. I will be your gardener."

Today, as always, I will walk to the shore to wait for you.

The Late-Blooming Flower *and Other Poems*

That fish over there!
It has no tail!

That flower over there!
It has no petals!

But look! The fish is swimming!
I swear it.
And the flower. It is opening!

Silver fish in a sea of petals,
garden of the moon.

Circa 1981

I'm Just Me

I'm just me,
I'm not out to please,
Just plain and simple, no frills attached,
Or titles onto which I latch.

Through all my life,
Through sunshine and rain,
I've done nothing
To claim any fame.

I've no string of accomplishments
That follow me around,
No awards, no honors
To which I resound.

My name's in no paper
Or magazine to boot,
There's no ambition
Towards which I shoot.

I'm Just Me

Though I'm not dressed
In the latest style,
I'm dressed just as well
As a crocodile.

I'm not fancy,
Or shmancy,
Or out to impress,
I just look my very best.

I'm Just Me

I was born into this world
Naked and free,
All just to be
Me Me Me.

What in the world is there else to be?
A president, a chief,
An idol, a star,
A heroine, a professor,
Or an alien from afar?

I think that's fine,
But for me at least,
All I ever wanted to be
Was just to be me.

I didn't have to try,
Couldn't learn it from a book,
Or hunt for buried treasure,
Just had to take a look.

There was nothing to do,
And nowhere to go,
No expert to guide me,
I was the whole show.

If you ask me for my secret,
Or wonder what is Me,
I honestly can tell you
I don't know.

And I'm certain that when I leave,
Taking nothing, not even my name,
My life will not
Have been lived in vain.

The world I've inhabited
Will never be the same
Because one, only one,
Song did I sing

That throughout the Universe
Sent forth its happy ring,
Just be me,
Just be me

So you just be you,
And I'll just be me.
Together let's fill the Earth
With gladness and glee.

Dedicated to my dear friend Janine Cooper Ayres,
Singer of many songs,
Who inspired this one

The Late-Blooming Flower *and Other Poems*

Nuances on Long-distance Friendship

a friend
miles that only my heart can cross

a friend
my heart
a long-distance flier

a friend
leaping over
mountains of miles

a friend
smiles clothed in words

a friend
photos of birds
land in my inbox

a friend
photos of birds
flutter to my inbox

a friend
photos of birds
singing in my inbox

A friend
miles evaporate

a friend
bird photos perch
on my inbox

a friend
connecting the dots
with words

a friend
I learn
to read braille

Dedicated to Tom Painting – poet, birder, teacher, friend, and to all the long-distance friends whose presence touches our lives

The Late-Blooming Flower *and Other Poems*

Unanswered

Babbling weeds whisper to the winds
    of
    winds and winged wine.

Imbibe the bitter honeysuckle
    of
    salted wetness
    and
    winded
    vines.

    Sighed
    broken
    stilled
    breaths

Matted straw whirls
    and
    falls
    Are echoes
    were weeds
whispering babbles of silence
    to
    stone.

January 1967

Ambling down a country lane one day,
I hardly noticed it where it lay
Among tall mustard leaves enshrouded
Where casually it had been discarded.

I wondered who the carpenter,
Perhaps a small boy,
And if his father stood by,
While he chiseled this little toy.

A simple design, two pieces of wood,
I do not know how long it stood,
Wings atop body secured together,
Olive-green paint long ago weathered.

We became fast friends, this plane and I,
And every time I wandered by,
Certain I was it awaited me,
Tacitly saluting in loyalty.

It was but yesterday, when scanning from afar,
I rushed to the place, my soul jarred,
The weeds had been sheared well-nigh to the ground,
And my little toy plane could nowhere be found.

Crestfallen, my steps slower paced,
Wondering, who the thief?
Had he picked it up in haste,
And like a useless weed,
Tossed it thoughtlessly into the waste?
Yet I hoped that perhaps he had a boy,
Who might delight in this small toy.

Though vanished forever from my sight,
My friend has taken another flight,
Soaring into my heart where it is enshrined,
This craft and I are securely entwined.

For Bill Norton, a pilot and friend to planes

The Late-Blooming Flower *and Other Poems*

Friendship

One day I asked a flower,
and then I asked a bee,
if they had ever heard of
Immortality.

I have, I told them bluntly,
and since you are my friends,
I wonder whether you will accompany me
to that place where there's no end.

We are too busy being here, replied,
and besides we're not invited,
to that impending sphere ethereal,
for mortals so material.

Then I told the flower,
and afterwards the bee,
that if they were excluded,
Immortality was not for me.

A Song of Solace

How Your heart must breaking be,
to receive unto your boundless sea
of Mercy and of Love,
the entreaties of multitudes, countless as the sands,
who gather at Your shore,
yet be impotent to stop
the braking of the tides –
rushing in just so far,
(a hope to linger),
then ebbing out to sea again
in obedient surrender!

The Late-Blooming Flower *and Other Poems*

You are only a memory now
It's as if you never existed
But suddenly I find I am
Drawn to you
Standing there in the snow
Filled with the freshness and
Wonder of it
I want to run to you
And bury myself in the
Warmth of your heart
But then I find in my hand
Only a picture that just once
Opened to the rain

June 1982

The Late-Blooming Flower *and Other Poems*

When you see
A flower
That is wilting,
Approach it gently,
Embrace it with water,
Shower it with kindness,
Serenade it with care.

Be careful
Not to step on it,
Trample it in a
Harsh storm of words,
Pronounce it guilty
Of a crime,
And imprison it
In the dark cell
Of your judgement.

You too are fragile
You too can wilt
You too need water

The flower is being
All that it can be,
Everything that it is.
It is shy.
It only asks for water.

Just give it water,
Unsparingly.
It is so simple.

Watch it unfold
In silent gratitude,
Blossoming in the sunshine
Of your attention,
Embracing you
In a shower
Of tender affection.

Just watch.

*Dedicated to my friend and mentor Jim McCormick,
who waters many flowers in the garden of music.*

Birthday Greeting

I am a butterfly of winter
My wings are gray
They carry many suns
Over there is my tightly gray-threaded house
From which I have just emerged
I look at it, with its tear I have rent
That will never be mended.
I once heard that butterflies came
Out in the summer, when
Many flowers bloomed.
I look about me.
All is bare.
I am alone; it is cold and I
Am trembling
I do not know what to do
I do not know where to go
I shall wait

The wind tears me from my twig.
I fly, I cannot go back.
In a gray empty field of crushed stalks
I discover, half-hidden, the orange flower of your absence
I gather its nectar
And send it to you for your birthday
All wrapped in a little white box
With an orange ribbon around it.
You will open it, and taste it,
Unknowingly,
And it will dance tenderly in your mouth
With the lingering sweetness of Brahms Waltz in Ab
That you have just taught me to play in a dream.

It will be just right,
As you said it was
(with the repeat soft and far away),
And the sweetness will seep,
Unknowingly, into your heart,
And come slowly from your eyes,
As you remember

February 1981

The Late-Blooming Flower *and Other Poems*

I didn't see her as she approached me
standing outside under a heat lamp
at a restaurant wearing a light
long-sleeved bright orange shirt
that looked stubbornly hot on a
cool and frigid night after the
heat of the day collapsed,
leaving me defenseless
to the cold.

My husband had spotted a
Thai restaurant surprisingly open
late at night in this unfamiliar town
as he was driving to our hotel some miles away.
A u turn landed us there,
hunger in our bellies,
cold in our bodies.
Cold feeds hunger,
Hunger feeds cold.
Common knowledge.
Experience teaches.

The restaurant was lively with business,
the air filled with good-natured conversation,
laughter, and the intermingling odors of delicious food.
My husband went inside to order.
I found a table outside,
standing as close to the overhead heat lamp
as I could, whose warmth approached the
radiation emanating from a single candle,
certainly not enough to warm a cold body
wearing a light long-sleeved shirt,
even if it was orange.
Despite the glow beaming directly
down at me,
I was shivering.
Instinctually I wrapped my arms around me.

She was a young woman,
seeming to appear out of nowhere
as she came up right beside me,
holding something in her hands.
"Here", she said, handing me a
thin but roomy gray fleece blanket
trimmed around the edges with black yarn.
"Take this."
"But isn't it yours?"
"Yes, but you can have it."
She promptly disappeared,
as mysteriously and suddenly
as she appeared.
I hungrily wrapped the blanket around my shoulders,
sheltering my body with its welcoming warmth,
deliciously smothered by the kindness of a stranger
who had become a lifelong friend.

When my husband came to the table
and saw the blanket enveloping me
like a cocoon, I told him how I
came to be wearing it.
He had on a short-sleeved shirt,
and was even colder than I had been.
Unhesitatingly, I removed the blanket
and placed it over his shoulders.
"You can have it", I said.
Of course, being a man
whose job it is to unflinchingly protect his wife,
he refused – at first.
But after I insisted,
he reluctantly but gratefully relented.
Role reversal is democratic.
One act of kindness handing itself to another,
like a blanket that while unfolding one section,
another is revealed, then another, without end.

The heat lamp became no more than redundant,
a convenient, though thoughtful device
set up for comfort.
That grey blanket warmed us bright orange.
It was more, much more, than a blanket
sheltering us from the cold,
which it still does.
It warmed us with the flame of compassion
turned into action,
coming from the inside out.

I will never forget that woman.
She is ever woven into the fabric of my life,
warming my heart with
the blanket of her kindness – even
on very cold nights.

The Garden

A man had a garden.
He loved his garden.
Every day he
Tended to his garden.
They sang songs to each other,
Songs of joy, sorrow, love, life, death.
Their songs were beautiful
Like a kaleidoscope of butterflies singing together.

One day a great war came.
There were men with guns and missiles,
Men full of hate
Who had no gardens.
He lost three friends,
One his best.
One day they aimed a missile at his home.
One deafening crash.
Then silence shattering everything.

The man lost all he had,
Mother, father, brother.
But the men of hate
Did not see his garden.
They could not kill it.
It remained.

But he could not remain
In the country of hate.
To a distant land he traveled,
Bringing his garden.
Every day he tends to his garden,
Singing songs to it.
In the new land his garden is blooming,
Singing of joy, sorrow,
Love, life, death,
And longing, and hope.

Passersby from many lands stop
To listen to the beautiful songs.
In their hearts many gardens bloom.
And they join with the man in song.

His garden is Music.

To music, the most pure of all languages,
Transcending and including all cultures.
And to Kayhan Kalhor,
Iranian musician, whose garden of music
Sings songs for all.

Society

The Late-Blooming Flower *and Other Poems*

Peace

For such a precious jewel,
Men journey far and wide,
Not seeing that to find it,
They have only to look inside.

The Late-Blooming Flower *and Other Poems*

Achievement is a tawdry thing,
A jewel in the crown of kings,
That once deposed from memory's throne,
Is cast into oblivion, unknown.

The Late-Blooming Flower *and Other Poems*

A Litany

Hate has
No place,
No race,
No color,
No space.

Descending
Like a plague
Of locusts
Swarming
With graffiti,
It defaces
Everything
In its path
With relentless
Wrath,

Displacing,
Erasing,
Effacing,
Encasing,
Alienating.

Hate perpetuates hate,
Has no mind,
Is never kind,
Is always blind.

It does not rhyme.
It does not rhyme.

A Curious Story

A breeze breathes gossip through the grass
Whispers spread in waves
Rumor ripples in the air
Trees bend their branches low to hear

All in chorus point a finger
The unison note is clear
Hurriedly scurries a squirrel by
Down into his hole he dives
The culprit must be near!

Lightning scars the distant sky
A shudder passes through the throng,
Sequel waiting tersely to clang along

The silence is unbearable,
an invisible scream,
But no percussion rumbles
the tightly sewn seam.

The breeze excuses stealthily,
never losing face
The trees lift their branches,
assuming proper place
The squirrel peers out cautiously,
then sidles out its hole,
And the grass, like a kitten,
unravels the green yarn of old.

Rap

Busy, busy, busy,
In a hurry,
In a hurry,
All wound up,
Full of worries;
Can't stop working,
got a long list to do,
got no time to listen to you.

Running, running, running,
got to keep apace,
list gets longer,
never win the race

Thirst gets stronger,
can't stop to drink,
can do nothing
but think, think, think

Parched is heart
that's drinking it's fill
of endless things
that it must do
(and never, not a moment,
to visit you).

Sun is rising in the sky
Got to do before I die

Sun is setting in the sky,
Got no time to say good-bye

The Late-Blooming Flower *and Other Poems*

Fame is so very slight a whim,
a feather in the cap of wind,
blowing up and blowing down,
then falling lightly to the ground.

The Late-Blooming Flower *and Other Poems*

pews compress so narrow a space,
universal amplitude cannot fit a place,
but patiently waiting like a faithful dog,
sits outside to offer grace

The Late-Blooming Flower *and Other Poems*

A house has many corners,
but none are fit to live,
save for an itinerant spider
in his hammock anchored,
like a craft that has been docked.

He reclines there soporific
waiting for his prey,
to snare as fish caught in a net
that nothing can allay.
Lazy, supine fellow! What an easy workaday!

Beware of human gossamer
in corners discreetly set,
that spinning so benign a trap,
danger will not notice,
till caught within its grasp!

A Whimsical Tale

It was one of those days
Where everything was rolling along without incident.
Children entered the room,
One by one,
Sat down at the piano,
Played their scales and arpeggios
Accompanied by an assortment of selections,
Demonstrating their pianistic skills
And interpretive style,

While I in my turn
hastily wrote comments
And marked appropriate boxes
Excellent, good, fair, fail,
As if everything shown to me
Could be caged within
A one-celled word.

Some were nervous,
Some poised,
Some prepared,
Others scared.

I tried to make them feel comfortable,
But I was officially crowned "The Judge",
A title I dearly wished to abdicate
For "A Listener".
But rules were rules.
No rubato allowed.

All was proceeding smoothly,
With clockwork precision,
As neat little chunks of
Pre-arranged time were
Skillfully pieced together
Like a mosaic.

In the midst of this musical inventory
A boy walks in,
Quite self-assured.
As usual, I asked for his music.
Without missing a beat he said,
"I forgot my music,
But I have my yo-yo",
As if this was the most natural thing
In the whole wide world.

Not missing a beat I said
(relieved that the tedium of routine
was broken,
And ready for some entertainment),
"Ok, show me some tricks
On your yo-yo."

Happily obliging,
He proceeded to unravel
A whole repertoire
Of virtuoso feats
On his instrument,
Pulling the string this way and that,
As though he was whisking through
Sets of scales and arpeggios.

My attention was galvanized,
Captured by that little boy
Who had spent hours perfecting his skills,
Diverting my focus from the fact
That he was a truant
Playing hooky for his delighted audience,
The Judge.

His performance?
Off the charts.

Years have since passed,
But I never forgot the little boy
Who so skillfully
Played the yo-yo for me.

I wonder what became of him.
Was his instrument lying unstrung, unsung,
Deftly tossed into a landfill,
Or stashed away in a box
Securely labeled "Childhood?"

Did he forsake his boyhood pleasures,
Succumbing to the lure of grown-up skills,
His attention wound around a screen,
Synthesizing charts and graphs and tables,
Pulling strings of numbers
Up and down,
Forwards and backwards,
Side to side,
Where you and I
Are lumped together in an assessment
Defined by our placement
On the rungs of a ladder of analysis?
I will never know.

But I harbor the hope
That his spirit is not wounded,
Wrapped tightly around a treadmill
Servile to grown-up expectation,
Afraid to release a string of tricks
For a delighted audience.

I relish the thought
That the man has not relinquished the boy,
That he is still buoyed up
By his boyish fun,
Playing the rascal
Abandoning strings of rules,
Captain at the helm
Of his ship of tricks,
From time to time veering off route,
Pulled by the strings
Of the whims
Of his heart.

Based on a true story

The Late-Blooming Flower *and Other Poems*

The Fabrication

Who would have thought
That such a lie
Could so seamlessly hide
Between fore and aft of man?

The tailor is clever,
The garment sleek;
So well-concealed is it,
You cannot take a peek.

So pleased was the craftsman
He patterned more,
Until he had amassed
A completely full store.

One day the town crier
Announced a fair.
Merchants came
To show their wares.

Crowds were clamoring
At the gates.
Expectation was terse,
They could hardly wait.

The gates were opened,
The mob rushed in,
Jostling each other,
Impatient to begin.

They browsed here, they browsed there,
Peering at the fare,
But for little, if nothing,
Did they care.

But when to the
Tailor's stand they came,
They stopped and stared,
Their mouths agape.

They had found what they sought,
Displayed in full array.
What did they buy?
The garments called Lies.

Two November Poems

Fame is like a meteor
Shooting across the sky,
Flashing for a moment,
Before it dies.

Build bridges, not barriers,
Though this may sound trite –
Doing one, but not the other,
Will end the world's plight.

An Oration

They are good people. Nice people.
Some of the nicest people you would ever want to meet.
They love their country.
They love their family.
They love their neighbor, as long as he agrees with them.

They will split your wood,
Bring you groceries,
Walk your dog,
Water your garden.
They are loyal to their friends. To the letter.
There is nothing they wouldn't do for them.

Upstanding citizens they are, too.
Obey the law. Good morals. Above board.
Contribute to charity.
Pro-gun and pro-life.
Their faith is unshakeable.
God is always on their side.

They love liberty. Worship freedom.
Freedom to do whatever they want.
It's a free country, they say. We the people.
No dictator dares tell them what to do. They have rights.
"Give me liberty or give me death!" is their motto.
"Don't tread on me!"

Wear a mask? , they say.
Not me. Nobody pushes me around.
I wouldn't be caught dead in one.
I'm no sissy.
I'd look silly.
God is protecting me.
What an inconvenience.
It doesn't feel good.
They lie to us. It's all a hoax.
I'm not contagious. Don't even have symptoms.
Scientists don't know the facts.
Masks? I can't breathe.
Only robbers wear masks.
Or raccoons.

They are good people. Nice people.
Some of the nicest people you would ever want to meet.

An old proverb says:
He who steals from another his liberty robs him of his life.
He who steals from another his life robs him of his liberty.
Do one, or do the other.
Both are acts of treason against Life.

(Every day, people are dying, their liberty gone,
Because a nice person refused to wear a mask.
It's their right.)

The Late-Blooming Flower *and Other Poems*

People of many talents
Neon the night with stars;
I prefer the fainter galaxies
Peopling the Universe from afar.

Their labors go unnoticed,
Their fields unseen,
But you and I could not sustain
Without the sustenance they maintain.

A Math Lesson

We all learned it in elementary school arithmetic.
Fractions.
The upper number is the numerator.
The lower number is the denominator.
There is a line in between the two.

If adding or subtracting
Two or more fractions
With different denominators,
Find the lowest common denominator.
Reduce large fractions
To the simplest terms.
For example,
16/20 = 4/5.

The rules make it easy
To work with large numbers.
Find what they have in common.
Reduce to simplest terms.
We understand this.

Here is an arithmetic problem:
Take numbers of people.
Billions.
Adding them up together
Equals the total sum
Of human beings on Earth.

Each is a fraction of the whole.
Each has a different numerator,
A different denominator.
Together, what is their
Lowest common denominator?

They differ in ages, sizes.
There are men, women,
Children, babies.
They all have bodies with
Nerves, brains, muscles, organs.
They feel happiness, sadness,
Grief, joy.
They eat, they sleep,
They think, they work,
They love, they hate.
They think a fraction
That has another denomination
Is an enemy.
Their denomination is peopled with
Fractions called friends.

These are the terms.
Now find the lowest common denominator.
Use logic.
It is clear, no matter what they call themselves,
All are doing and feeling similar things.
Where is the difference?
The LCD is each of them together.
Reduce the fraction to
Its simplest terms.
This is you and me.
Don't let appearances fool you.
Underneath the mask
Is a human being.
All the fractions
Reduced to the simplest term.
No strangers, no outliers, no wild cards.
Elementary math.
Elemental.

A moment ago,
A woman was preparing breakfast
In her apartment.
Her building was divided
Into many apartments.
Each a fraction.
She was talking to her fiancée
About their wedding,
Just a month from now.
Her face was lit up with joy.

A moment later,
The building burst into flames.
Hit by a bomb.
An avalanche of rubble.
A shrapnel of fractions.
In an instant,
Joy blotted out.
The murkiness of murder.
A wedding canceled.

All because of bad math.
They, the perpetrators,
Had missed the mark,
Aiming at a jumble of fractions
With no LCD,
Reducing them to their simplest terms,
A pile of chaos, a remainder of grief.
They failed at solving a simple arithmetic problem.

Whoever instructed mankind to
"Love your neighbor as yourself"
Was a good math teacher.
But the students didn't learn.
As yourself = same as yourself,
Sharing the lowest common denominator,
Reduced to the simplest terms.
1/1 = 1

A Search

It was a blustery fall day, cold and uninviting. Thousands of leaves were raining down from the trees, piling up silently on the ground. I was inside, snuggled up before a cozy warm fire, casually leafing through a large catalogue. Being rather old-fashioned, I like catalogues, the feel of them, the texture of the paper, the turning of the pages, one by one. I was scouting through each page trying to find something I was looking for, like a detective attempting to unearth a piece of a puzzle. I turned one page, then another, and another, dazzled by the sheer array of gadgets and devices and what-have-you's that could fix any problem one encountered. They were all displayed in neat little boxes accompanied by neat little descriptions, like so many flowers coyly displaying their wares in the hope of attracting bees.

I was certain that somewhere amongst all of these hundreds of articles, I would find what I was looking for. Everything was advertised as new and improved, exactly what I wanted. I was on the right track, on the verge of a discovery.

There were new and improved toasters, hair dryers, vacuum cleaners, computers, keyboards, laundry detergents, tractors, bicycles, wood-burning stoves, plumbing supplies, refrigerators, water pumps, blenders, cleaners, kitchen utensils, light bulbs, phones. The list went on and on. But what really amazed me were the robots – robots to do your laundry, clean your house, babysit your kids, be your companion, and fix your car. Everything was designed to make life easier in order to gain more leisure time. Imagine! Hundreds of slaves to do your bidding. No king or queen ever had it better.

But I had no desire to invite these assistants into my living space. I was determined to find something else. I'm content with the devices I have. They work. They were made to last year after year, like an old tree.

I thought back to a time, over two million years ago, when human ingenuity discovered that a rock could be turned into a tool. Imagine the joy that lit up that first inventor's face! A new and improved way of accomplishing a task. Instantly, life was made easier. Year after year, invention followed invention, in exponential leaps and bounds, and the old was discarded for the new and improved.

I resumed turning pages until, after a couple of hours, I arrived at the end of the catalogue. In spite of all my meticulous sleuthing, what I was looking for was nowhere to be found. Apparently no-one had been clever enough to invent it. Perhaps I am being foolish, I thought to myself, to entertain the notion that, in our advanced technological era, someone, somewhere would have the wherewithal to invent what I sought – a new and improved human being. Wouldn't this invention solve more problems than all the devices in the world?

Homo sapiens pride themselves on being the most intelligent creatures on planet Earth. From identifying a simple rock as a tool, they have progressed so far that they can now probe outer space. Yet all the while their backs are turned on the fact that they are the most destructive species, earning for them the dubious title of being the most dangerous.

Intelligence has its shortcomings, though, as humans are incessantly complaining about how hard their lives are, despite all the gadgets they have. If I'm not mistaken, homo sapiens are the only creatures on Earth that complain.

Punctuating history is the inexorable march of war, famine, violence, poverty, and disease. The little things invade between the cracks like an army of ants – annoyances, arguments, disagreements, misunderstandings, unfulfilled desires – tears in the fabric of Life.

Piercing through the complaining is the drumming mantra "there's never enough time in the day to do everything I want to do"! Never enough time, even with all the labor-saving devices working away. A conundrum that in the same breath races to push forward while backtracking.

To top it all off, humans bemoan the fact that they are lonely. There is no time in the day to spend with each other. They are too busy spending time with their devices, which spend time chattering with each other. That precious attribute of humanity, the unique voice which each and every person possesses, is becoming more and more a rarity. It is being drowned out by that voracious non-native bird of prey – email, accompanied by a flock of twitters and tweets.

Many have tried to re-form the "old" human being, pumping knowledge into him gleaned from myriad spiritual pursuits, meditation, psychology, and a plethora of self-improvement manuals. But after all the advice and urgings of experts, has slavishly following this path or that ever led to a complete and revolutionary change? After trying on all sorts of new garments, is the emperor still denying the fact that he is wearing no clothes?

I thought of an old adage that states "Necessity is the mother of invention". But with the need ever-present to create a new and improved human being, why hadn't the mother ever given birth?

Maybe, I mused, just maybe, this was an impossible task, like climbing up an apple tree to find a pear. That with all the knowledge encased in the walled pyramid of Time, none of it was enough to formulate an invention that was capable of completely transforming mankind. Knowledge has limits, which it constantly surpasses, but going beyond one border only creates another border. Complete change, I thought, happens when there is no residue left of the past, which is knowledge.

I closed the catalogue and looked at the fire. The bright orange flames were leaping and twirling in a strange, seductive dance. Fueled by old wood, they were carousing wildly, as the logs upon which they fed were being destroyed until reduced to ashes. The flames were not seeking to change the wood, transforming it into something new and improved. They were simply burning.

Something stirred within me, something new and unfamiliar, leaping up from deep inside me. An insight which dictated the end to all my searching. "To seek change is not to change."

It occurred to me that mankind, with his sights set on outer space, could turn his energy toward exploring inner space. What great mysteries would be unearthed! But in such uncharted territory, could anyone lead the way? There was no map, no compass, on which to rely. Each one was utterly alone in his journey.

I looked outside at the trees, their branches bare of leaves, which prompted by the wind, had scattered in all directions and lay fallen on the ground like interlocking pieces of an intricate puzzle. The wind had not sought to create in its wake a forest of trees barren of leaves. It had just blown, unseen.

The wind, I suddenly realized, had stopped. I decided to depart from the comfort zone I had settled into and venture outside. The cold air was unsettling, but fresh and invigorating. I remembered how, as a child, I had loved to play in the mounds of dead leaves, jumping into them and hearing them crunch. Propelled by that memory, I jumped joyously into the leaves, marching through them, listening with delight to their familiar yet unfamiliar sound. That was years ago. I am still marching through the leaves. Still listening . . . .

The Late-Blooming Flower *and Other Poems*

A Narrative

It was so simple.
So absurdly simple.

He walked into
A gun shop,
Bought a gun
And walked out.

The next day
He walked into
A grocery store,
Killed ten people.

Shots were scattered,
Lives were shattered,
Bodies lay strewn
Across the room.
He was apprehended,
Taken into custody,
His motives dissected,
His background suspected.

Victims were identified,
Bodies lay cold,
Multitudes were mortified,
Grief took hold.

Time was adjourned
Terror held reign,
Smiles were defiled
By blood-tainted pain.

Families were broken
By their losses,
Only shards remained
In memory's lane.

Chasms of emptiness
Filled with tears,
Missing loved ones
Who were dear.

Never to see,
Never to hear,
Never to hug,
Never to heal.

Funerals were held,
Eulogies were read,
Wreaths were laid
For the dead.

All for naught
Ten mortals shot.

Hordes that sobbed
Will turn away,
Laws curbing firearms
Hold no sway.

Hate will proliferate
Obeying the rules,
Conforming to will
Weapons will kill.

Doors pursue revolving
Around and around,
Hounded are arms,
Screams will sound.

Life limps along
On one-legged crutches,
Lives are pawned
For selfdom's clutches.

It's so easy.
Easy as 1-2-3.

A man walks
Into a store,
Buys a gun,
Shuts the door.

Dedicated to the victims of the Boulder, Colorado grocery store murders
March 22, 2021,
and all future victims of gun violence

A Cautionary Tale

I've got to do it,
Got to do it,
Before it's too late.

Got to do it,
Got to do it,
Every chance I'll take.

I'll comb the skies
For butterflies,
Soaring above the clouds,

Take a plane
To every place
Save for outer space.

They'll never call me
Stay-at-home Charlie
Sitting on a chair,

Munching chips
All day long
In my comfy lair.

I'll take a thousand selfies
And post them to a screen,
Of all the places I've been to
That you have never seen.

North, South,
East, West,
I'll conquer them all.

And while
I am at it,
I'll just have a ball,

Wining and dining
And seeing the sights,
In every outpost
Where I alight.

Mountains and valleys,
Cities and towns,
Seducing one, then another,
As did Don Juan.

But trust me,
I'm not selfish,
I recycle all the trash,
Paper and plastic,
Down to the last scrap.

Soda cans, beer bottles,
Copper and tin,
All find their way
Into my bin.
I refuse to
Trash the Earth
As long as I last.

I listen to the experts,
Who tell me not to fly,
'Cause planes heat-trapping gases
Are more than is wise.

They say that
The air is foul,
The Earth is in heat,

But I'm vying
For the world's record
And I won't be beat.

I've got to jet-hop
From one place to the next,
Going faster and faster
From East to West.

Else how can I
My mission achieve,
To see every country
Before I leave?

Hell, I'm just one person,
What harm can I do,
If the Earth warms a little,
They won't have a clue.

Besides, I have a right
To happiness pursue.
Me? Not me.
I won't be trapped.
A majority of One
Is the total sum.

The Late-Blooming Flower *and Other Poems*

Nuances on New Year's Day

New Year's Day
family visit to
the nursing home

New Year's Day
caring for her
husband with Alzheimers

New Year's Day
well-wishers
visit the hospital

New Year's Day
branches sparkling
with yesterday's rain

New Year's resolution
the leaves can
wait another day

New Year's Day
the rake's in
the garage

New Year's Day
no holiday
for birds

New Year's Day
the calendar's crowded
with birthdays

New Year's Day
absence

New Year's Day
blank spaces
for funerals

New Year's Day
counting the days
to summer vacation

New Year's Day
to-do lists waiting
to be filled

New Year's Day
silence at the
construction site

New Year's Day
the Earth isn't
stopping to celebrate

Turning Point

A door has hinges;
One way opens,
the other closes.
What happens if you
stand on one side,
and I on the other?
One grasps firmly
the knob to open,
the other to hold it shut.

The door cannot move.
Arguments, shouting, pounding,
Wrestling of wills.

Movement has no obstruction;
Like water, it finds its way
Resist, and you are at war.

Through a door you cannot see
Each side mirrors the other
Both are sides
Seeing this, can you let go
of your grasp?
If so, with great ceremony
remove the door
Bow to the mirror of yourself.
Then where are the sides?

Freely pass through
Breathe in, breathe out
No hinges

Folksong – A Veteran's Tale

I fought for my country when I was good and strong
They said it wouldn't last too long
They told me killing is all right
I believed they couldn't be wrong

They say they want peace, but fight a war
There ain't no ceiling and ain't no floor
Protecting our land is at the core
Else our country would be no more

They ordered me to destroy the enemy
I blasted them all to eternity
Then one day something hit me
Blew my legs off one, two, three

I served my country, yesiree,
But they never told me how my country would serve me
They gave me a medal and gave me a chair
And didn't ask once how I would fare

But the pain's so bad I can hardly sit down
And on my face I wear a frown
The medal – I buried it underground
It's all I can do to wheel around town

I can't help but see the terror in the eyes
Of those whom I shot at, caused to die
And be haunted by families stricken with grief
Stranded in a wasteland like boats that have been beached

So now I have no other aim
Than to live in a country without a name
Where fences of thought that keep us apart
Dissolve to the beat of our human heart

Abstractions are daunting,
They loom like towering peaks,
Or deepest depths of oceans,
That only scholars seek.

My simple mind can't fathom
The temerity of such,
That to superior places
Send their feet to touch.

"The World" is beyond me,
"Society" the same,
But defined in thoughts and actions,
They are our domain.

Dedicated to Jiddu Krishnamurti (1895-1986),
Who in his teachings said, "You are the World".

A Note on Devices

Recently I saw a cartoon by the great Australian cartoonist Michael Leunig.

It depicted a beautiful tree full of pink blossoms in the spring. Beside the tree, and facing away from it, was a man in profile intently watching a device. The caption under the cartoon read: "The Miracle of Spring — Man Looking at Football Game on his Device."

Although devices have their place as useful tools, are they not destroying true face-to-face social interaction, and voice-to-voice contact infused with a person's spirit? I think they create the illusion of contact at your fingertips, but the word "contact" really implies "touch," to literally be "in touch." Illusion is pleasant and safe, but it can never be a substitute for the real thing.

Machines are vehicles of convenience and expediency, but I don't see people any happier as a result of devoting so much time, energy, and money to them. I actually think that they and their use are contributing to widespread alienation and loneliness.

People can be sitting next to each other in a restaurant, other public places, even at home, eyes glued to their respective devices, looking fearful and anxious lest they miss a message or text. They feel connected, but to what? Or, in the alternative, is the machine a modern-day piece of armor shielding them from the vagaries of direct contact?

Just as the Earth is losing biodiversity, human beings are losing diversity of experience. Bookstores and record stores are mostly gone. Like falling dominoes, many other enterprises are following.

In their place? Ipods, Kindle, Nook, the all encompassing Amazon, and downloads with their poor sound quality. Again, we are losing touch with the individual feel of a book or recording, holding it in our hands, and putting it lovingly on a shelf, perhaps to be used again, or shared with an interested friend.

Loss of jobs, loss of social interaction becomes the collateral damage of lost diversity. Perhaps people have lost jobs they actually enjoyed, because on some level they were directly sharing valuable and sometimes personal information and experience with their customers. Would outsourcing be as efficient and profitable without all the devices which make instant communications possible?

Is there a real value in silence and space outside of the incessant chatter and texting on cell phones that is epidemic in our society? Once I was picking cherries in an orchard in Leona Valley, when suddenly the peace and beauty of it all was interrupted by a cell phone conversation.

Whatever happened to privacy? I, for one, do not want to be privy to someone's private life in a grocery store setting. With the volume turned on high, the cell phone user often seems oblivious to his or her surroundings.

Does all this "need to be connected" stem from a deep-rooted loneliness, which, by plugging into devices, can provide what seems to be a "fix?" But, because devices cannot cure loneliness, with its underlying fear of isolation, a pattern of dependency develops, resulting in addiction.

Loneliness implies a state of "feeling separated from," whereas the root of the word "alone" is "all one."

What would happen if everyone unplugged for a day? A neighbor told me a rather amusing story. One day he was sitting next to his boss at work, who said, "I just emailed you." My neighbor said, "Can't you just tell me?" "No," the boss replied. "I emailed you."

Obesity is a major problem in our culture. Surely, outside of other factors, the overuse of devices which encourage a sedentary lifestyle contributes greatly to becoming overweight. Messages are sent via email rather than walking to a co-workers station.

A couple of months ago I tried to phone a professor at his local college. The message on his phone was as follows: "Please do not leave a message. Email me." Enough said. I never talked to him.

I am device free, except for one landline phone and limited computer use. I feel unencumbered, simple and happy in this way. I communicate with friends either by phone, in person, or by letter written in handwriting which conveys my personality in the moment. I enjoy the delicious anticipation of waiting for something.

Whether in my garden or on frequent hikes, I feel part of the ever changing rhythms, harmonies, colors and sounds of nature. I feel truly fortunate to live in a community where "Nature is our neighbor". I do not feel deprived and get along quite well in this world.

The observations in this article are by no means an attempt to "convert" others to my way of life. Devices are here to stay. They are a valuable and indispensable resource in many arenas. They can and do link people together in vital ways. Although I do not have them at home, many activities I engage in would be impossible without them.

Yet the question remains: Has society gone overboard in its obsessive, frenzied attachment to these new electronic toys of civilization? Armed with our newly born powers of omniscience and omnipresence have we lost something vital, and like unwitting prey lie caught in a web of our own making?

What are we here for? I think it is to be with each other. By expressing our uniqueness in relationships, which includes nature, in an embrace of respect, appreciation and care, we become truly human. We are not machines, and machines cannot replace us. Making human beings our first priority is to put devices in their proper perspective.

Linda Love
Elizabeth Lake, California
Guest Editorial – *The Mountain Yodeler*, July, 2012

The Late-Blooming Flower *and Other Poems*

Evolution

There's a person in the room next door,
I hardly ever see his face,
He sends me thirty emails a day,
It's as if I were erased.

He sits in his lair in a comfy chair
Fixated on his task,
Though a reprieve of minutes
Is all I'd ever ask.

Though the distance between us
Is only a few feet to pace,
It would be more accurate to say
He was occupying outer space.

I suppose that as members of the human race
We've come a very long ways
Since the time when neighbors who lived next door
Talked to each other face to face.

But as for me,
With my antiquated ways,
I think I'd rather be a Neanderthal
Than greet a fellow human
Hardly at all.

The Late-Blooming Flower *and Other Poems*

Refrain

She caught my attention, walking down the street
Looking at her phone,
Head bowed down,
Body hunched over.

Feeling friendly, I said hi to her. No response, she
Looking at her phone,
Head bowed down,
Body hunched over.

Again I greeted her. Hi there!
Oblivious to my presence, she went her way,
Looking at her phone,
Head bowed down,
Body hunched over.

Thousands of leaves were shining in the sunlight,
Golden grasses rustling in the breeze,
Insects humming, birds singing,
Sunflowers nodding their bright yellow heads to and fro.

Ever faithful, a devout worshipper,
She never lifted her eyes,
Looking at her phone,
Head bowed down,
Body hunched over.

A curious sight to behold,
Like a meandering mummy encased in a cocoon,
From which no butterfly would emerge,
Warm its wings,
And take flight.

Intent on not missing anything.
Missing everything.
A prisoner of technology,
Magnetized by the alchemy of her device.
Locked in a cell.
Sentenced to solitary confinement.

Truth be told, I should mention that I approached her one more time.
Just because.
Hi! , I called out, not holding my breath.
Just for one moment – one moment – she glanced up at me
(I think more to ward off my persistence than anything else)
And tossing the ball back to me
That I had thrown to her
Answered with the requisite hi,
Dismissing me promptly
As though I were an annoying interruption
To her hypnotic trance,
Then immediately resuming her pose,
Looked at her phone,
Head bowed down,
Body hunched over.

On past me she walked,
Disappearing into her phantom cloud.
The conversation?
Ended.

It's a wonder she didn't stumble over
The big pine cones scattered
Across the road.
There were so many towering pine trees overhead.

It's a wonder.

Adjournment

He asked them to leave.
Politely, of course.
Remove Yourselves
And Your Belongings.
You have 48 hours to Vacate Everything
But Clean Dirt.

Their encampment was taboo.
They were taboo.
The riff-raff. The rubbish.
The untouchables. The outcasts.
The scum of the earth.
Epithets.

But he did not say that.
Never mentioned that
The neighbors had complained,
Complained of the stench,
The filth, the trash.

The neighbors who lived
In nice houses with tidy lawns
And rosebushes
In a respectable neighborhood,
Who went to work every morning
And returned home every evening,
Whose children were forbidden
To play with "their" children
Because they were dirty.

The neighbors who held their noses
And averted their eyes full of fear
As they walked by hunched over
With embarrassment
At the human blunder that had
Stumbled onto their path.

It was all for a good cause,
Neighborhood Cleansing,
That they wrote the letters, made the phone calls,
Attended meetings, made their voices heard,
They, the good citizens of Anytown, USA.

The town council listened.
They listened with 50 pairs of ears
To the uproar, to the tumult,
Of the respectable citizens
Pleading with them to do something
To relieve them
Of the unsightly heap of human garbage
Fouling up their lives.

The meeting was adjourned.
The good burghers consented,
Capitulating to their pressing demands
Like falling dominoes,
Voting unanimously
In favor of a 48 hour eviction notice.
A clean sweep. No mercy.
Not that it was that difficult.

But not one of "them" had been invited to speak,
The disenfranchised, voiceless diaspora of humanity.
Not one of "them" had been given the slightest chance
To tell how they worked years from morning to night
To live on meager wages
In a meager house
And eat meager food
Until they lost their jobs
And couldn't pay the mortgage,
Or the landlord raised the rent
And their wages couldn't climb that high.

Given a three-day eviction notice, they were.
All doors locked behind them.
No questions asked. No questions answered.
Suddenly nameless, faceless,
Uprooted, chastised, homeless,
Drifting from one place to another
Like sands in a desert.
Gypsies,
Staring with vacant eyes
Into a vacant lot.

While right in the public eye,
Billions are spent on weapons,
Millions are spent on luxury homes
And luxury vacations,
Thousands are spent on frivolous litigations
And political affiliations.

But they, the drifters, the shiftless,
Were not worthy of a dime,
Sunk in the quagmire of quicksand
Sucking them beneath respect,
Stripping them of even a dime's worth of dignity.

And so it happened on a
Bright and sunny day
That the anointed one
Handed them the notice.
No questions asked. No questions answered.
48 hours to get out of their encampment.
Period.

It was nobody's business where they would go.
Theirs was a portable ghetto.
It could relocate.
Anywhere but here.
Only the unborn weeds that were
Certain to crop up
In the wake of their departure,
Only they were allowed to remain.

The next day a trash truck came by
To pick up an old broken-down piano
That had been ordered to vacate its music.

Closure.

*Based on a true story
on the liquidation of a homeless encampment
in Portland, Oregon*

The Late-Blooming Flower *and Other Poems*

Masked in medieval armor, you, on your steed of steel
who brandish a fearsome lance and shield,
I am no match for you.

My lance is a blade of grass,
my shield a yellow daisy,
my armor the shadow of an apple tree,
my horse a billowy cloud.

Appearing, I disappear,
my rhythms are untrained,
knowing neither conquest nor captivity,
what stance can I maintain?

Where can you find me, on your steed of steel?
What battle to fight? To what end?
I am no match for you, my friend.

A Wish

His name is Aiden.
He is nine years old.
He is in fourth grade.
He is a beginning piano student.

We have lessons on Zoom.
It isn't easy.
You know how it is.
We are in a pandemic.
Social distancing.
Miles away.
We are safe.

He goes fast.
He is a boy.
He stumbles many times.
He gets frustrated.
He can't hide it.
His body language
Gives it away.

I tell him
That the fastest way to learn
Is to go slow.
It gives his brain a clear message.
His brain sends the message instantly
To his nerves and muscles.
Something like sending an email.
It arrives in a flash.
No delays.

Going too fast
And stumbling
Is like trying
To climb a slippery slope.
You keep
Sliding backwards
And never get anywhere.

He is learning.
He tries going slow.
His body yields to triumph.
It works!
The tortoise wins the race.
The hare is left behind.
Near the end of his lesson
We have a make-up-a song-time.
It's like a conversation.
He makes up a song,
I make up a song.

He is adventuresome.
Not afraid to try new sounds.
He doesn't know a lot about music.
Not knowing, he feels free.

No-one is telling him
What belongs together,
What doesn't belong together.
He has no well-trodden paths to follow.
He explores, untethered by rules.

His fingers make up sentences.
The sentences tell stories.
I guess what they are,
Like in a game of charades,
Only the characters are cloaked in tunes.

This week his story
Sounded angry.
I told him so.
His right hand was playing triads
In the upper register.
His left hand answered with triads
In the lower register.

I've explained to him what triads are.
Three notes played at the same time,
Like a word typed with one space
Between each letter.
Resembling a happy family,
Together they make harmony.

A big gap separates his hands.
Nothing in between.
The threesomes hold their ground
On opposite ends of the keyboard.
No meeting place.
Loud clanging chords.
A series of three simultaneous sounds,
Followed by other sets of three.
Never together.

The happy families group themselves
At polar ends.
They call themselves by different names.
They do not hear that each of them
Is a happy family.
They clash.
There is a battle.
Some die.
The happy families are sad.

Angry.
I think my
guess was on the mark.

"So, Aiden, what was your song about?"
"It was a fight", he replied.
"Yes", I said. "It sounded like that."
"There's too much fighting in the world, isn't there?"
"Yes", he said.
He is nine years old.
He already knows this age old fact of life.

Then his face brightened. He smiled.
"I wish everybody would have fun,
And that the only fighting
Would be piano fights."

I was stunned.
Tears came.

Aiden is a boy.
He is nine years old.
He likes to have fun.
Having fun is having fun.
No room for fighting.
No room for war.
Room for smiles and laughter.
Only.

He has found the solution
To the world's problems.
Not that he ever looked for it.
He doesn't have to think about it.
He does not offer an opinion.
He doesn't pen a law.
He doesn't sign a peace treaty.
No-one gives him the answer.
He knows.
It's so easy.
Just have fun.

Dedicated to Aiden,
And all the children and grown-ups
Who like to have fun.

The Late-Blooming Flower *and Other Poems*

An Inquiry

Alaina is Aiden's sister.
She is eight years old.
Delicate looking.
Long straight black hair.
She has the self-assuredness that comes from
Having a good home, good parents,
A nice (well, most of the time) brother,
Three cats, a dog,
And 1000 stuffed animals.
I tell her that I like stuffed animals, too,
And even have some snakes.
Her eyes open wide.
We bond.

She is my piano student.
Zoom, of course.
The lingering side effects of the pandemic.
The sound zooms out unannounced every lesson.
She's frustrated, I'm frustrated.
Every new device devised to make life easier
Comes with a set of problems
That make it difficult.
She tries to fix it. An apprentice mechanic.
The sound returns. The problem is fixed.

We are happy. The lesson resumes.
Again the sound crashes.
I say, "Call your dad." It's the default solution.
Dad enters. He fixes it.
Not understanding what he did,
I conclude that he must be some kind of sorcerer.
Meanwhile, her lesson time is ticking away
Like a wound-up metronome winding down.

Alaina has an ongoing problem
Turning her thumb under playing scales.
We only have five fingers on each hand.
Something has to give somewhere
If we want to travel farther than five keys.
So we have to turn the thumb under
Or cross a finger over.
Many borders are crossed. No passport needed.

"Be prepared", I tell her.
"Turn your thumb under early.
It will go smoothly, no bumps."
She tries. She misses.
"Alaina, do you know that
I'm not the best teacher for you? You are."
She looks at me, a puzzled expression on her face.
I go on. "The key to learning is attention.
Attention means to be present, in attendance.
Like when the teacher calls your name in rollcall,
You raise your hand and answer "Here".
When you give attention to what you are doing,
You are teaching yourself."
Alaina smiles. She seems to grow a few inches.
She attends. Her thumb obeys.

Today Alaina is wearing a tee-shirt
The color of raspberry sherbet.
In big letters on the front it proclaims
"Smart Girls Rule The World".
I ask her if she is smart.
She nods her head, with a surety impossible to conceal.
Going out on a limb,
(after all, this is supposed to be a piano lesson)
I ask her, "What would you do if you ruled the World?"

She thinks for a moment.
Her little face takes on a pained expression.
"I think it's terrible that there are so many homeless people",
She says in an exasperated tone.
"I have a nice home, a roof over my head,
Enough to eat, nice parents.
(and 1000 stuffed animals).
"Why should there be kids who are
Younger than me, older than me,
Who don't have a home?
Why should there be?!!"
As she speaks, she raises her arms up and down
To show me how little, how big, the kids are.

I'm speechless.
She does not understand how life can be so unfair.
I can't help her there. I don't understand, either.
She continues.
"If I had a lot of money, I would give it to homeless people.
Here, have some money,
Here, have some money.
Here, have some money."
She gestures with her hands, throwing them out,
Opening her palms.

I am astonished.
Yes, she is smart.
But much more than that,
She has a big heart.
She contemplates beyond
The four walls of her comfortable house.
Her heart houses the homeless.
She would attend to them.
I think that qualifies her to rule the world.
She would rule not only with her head,
But with her heart.
A winning combination.

I have a thought to nominate her
For Ruler of the World.
I would be her campaign manager.
She has a good platform,
And I have just the right slogan for her crusade.
"Vote for Alaina, the little girl with the big heart!"

*For Alaina, and everyone who reaches out and beyond
four walls and five fingers
(and likes stuffed animals)*

The Late-Blooming Flower *and Other Poems*

Life and Death

Ideals are virtues
Placed high on a shelf;
Between words and actions –
How enormous the gulf.

A reconciliation pursued shall never meet,
Just as a child's hands,
Aspiring to reach a hidden jar of sweets,
Will always rest beneath.

If

"If's" a bit uncertain,
A wanton, wily thing,
Yet on its frayed and well-worn rope,
Many, suspended, swing!

The Late-Blooming Flower *and Other Poems*

Disowned

The morphology of physic*
Is undeniably abstruse;
I search the hieroglyphic –
Myself is out of use.

*an archaic word for medicine

In Search of a Prayer

God, and Peace, and Truth, and Love
Oh, they are caught in corners,
Enmeshed in spiders webs
Whence History summons
With clarion calls and lyres.

They fall to their knees
In front of these cherished idols,
These lying looms of love crying
God, give us Peace, give us peace.

Silly fools! The sun unmasks me
To look inside
And find the self that there resides;
Truth follows truth in woods
Where shadows are light ……..

January 1967

Goliath Versus David

How strange it is
so small a thing
should cause so large a fright;
the body meets it's enemy
and prepares to flee or fight
the muscles tauten testily
the throat lets out a gasp
or screams emerge volcanic
from a steaming cauldron vast

The creature conceals a demon,
a devil in disguise,
how can it look so guileless,
unaware of coming demise?

The strategist consults
with superior domain
the multitude of weapons
that dominate its brain,
then choosing one
stalks its prey
with carefully calculated aim

Bending to the task,
as bow is to arrow,
the distance between
cautiously narrows

Down swats the discordant perfidious blow,
dooming the creature to nothing but woe.

Nothing is heard
but buzzing of wings,
wanton disgrace
to defeated chase.

There is the devil,
aloft upside-down,
nimbly acrobatic,
innocent as a clown

Hulk defeated by
natural design,
Goliath retreats sullen
from rapacious reign.

Agile victor in the claim
 (once again prone),
David crowned King
assumes the throne.

The Late-Blooming Flower *and Other Poems*

Epitaph

The birds have stopped their singing
Silence is white as snow
Quiet spreads its breathless wings
The rest we do not know

from an inscription
    found on an ancient ruin

    What is visible fades away;
    the invisible is here to stay,
    like treasure buried beneath the ground,
    that with map and compass can never be found.

The Late-Blooming Flower *and Other Poems*

Immortality is a word
By wizardry conjured,
Preached from every pulpit
Yet never seen nor heard.

Requiring only faith,
The exchange a priceless thing,
The most who are impoverished
Trade gravity for wings.

The belief assuages all lament,
Tethering hope to discontent.
Perched on a fulcrum between heaven and hell,
The trajectory assures that no-one ever tells.

Leavetaking

Motionless, we pause at death,
then monument of stone erect.
We shed our flowers, hesitate,
then grief shuttering, resurrect.

Wrenched from life,
we molt to streets,
wheels grinding ceaselessly
earth to concrete.

Immersed in traffic
turning round and round,
a cacophony of rain
tumbles noiselessly to the ground.

The Late-Blooming Flower *and Other Poems*

I had a vision of my life,
and then it blew away,
like a shiny soap bubble
in a little round holder
that delights a child's play.

The Late-Blooming Flower *and Other Poems*

A Snapshot

It is not a birthday party,
A family reunion,
A yearbook page,
A graduation

Not a class picture,
A summer camp,
A club,
A choir,
Or a fond memento cached away.

It is none of these.

Scissored neatly out of a newspaper,
Yellowed with age,
Carefully folded,
This photo tucked inside
The front cover of a book.

It's a bright and sunny day.
Children are grouped in front
Of a tall, rickety stick fence,
Like a grove of young saplings,
Their bare feet planted
On the bare ground.

Some girls, some boys,
Loosely arranged in rows,
Tallest to shortest,
Hair cut short,
Some light, some dark.

Serious,
That tall boy in the back with glasses.
Perplexed,
The boy next to him.
Robust,
The boy to his side.
Confused,
The boy in the middle.
That taller boy next to him,
Defiant.
Smiling,
A friendly boy adjacent to him.
Wondering,
The tall boy bookending the back row.

Sweetly looking,
The little fellow in front
Of the tall boy with glasses.
Uncomfortable,
The short boy in the second row.
Hidden,
A child behind another.
Grinning,
That cute boy with his ears sticking out.
Endearing,
This smiling little boy neighboring him.
Mysterious,
The girl with shadowed eyes
In front of him.

Apprehensive, distrustful,
The little girl in a blouse and jumper.
Winsome,
A blonde-haired boy next to her.
The last child,
Arms raised,
A tiny girl covering her eyes with her hands,
Crying.

A catalogue of 16,
A tribe of children orphaned from their parents,
Their soon-to-be obliterated names
Vanishing in wispy highways
Of smoke,
Memorialized by an unseen cameraman
Lurking behind his instrument.

Not just any children, these.
They are Jewish children,
Hand-picked.
Singled out for special treatment.

Saved for the record.
Saved together in one single
Snapshot,
The last one,
Their final portrait,
Taken right before their execution,
Their endearing faces
And diminutive bodies
Adorned in shabby clothes,
Etched on film
For all posterity to view.

The remnants of a family,
A birthday party,
A class,
A camp,
A club,
A choir,
Their voices silenced,
Gunned down,
Stricken fledglings
Fallen from the nest of life,
Never given a chance to fly.

Why did the photographer snap them
In the jaws of his camera?
Was it for a publicity shot?
To be honored with a badge for his heroism?
Or perhaps for a trophy to hang on a wall,
Something to send home
To his wife and children?

To be sure,
The hunter regaled in his catch,
His copse of corpses,
Felled by his orderly barrage of bullets.
To be sure,
His compatriots pat him on the back,
Praised him for a job well done.
No doubt he was hailed as a hero,
His picture in all the papers.
And for what?
For having rid the Earth
Of the scourge of
16 Jewish children.

Permit me to interject this postscript:
If only, if only,
I could have hovered
Over these children,
Sheltered them fiercely
With wings of Love,
And borne them to a far-away island,
Safe from their indifferent predator.

But I am only left
With a poverty of words,
A futile trail of crumbs
Leading nowhere but to
A skeleton of lifeless memory,
An empty space
In front of
A rickety fence of sticks.

Dedicated to each of the 1.5 million children
Murdered in the Holocaust

Shopping

Life is not a bargain.
You can't buy it on sale.
You either
Take it as it is
Or leave it.
You don't have a choice of
Hundreds of brands to choose from.

You can't argue
With the salesperson,
Or propose a barter.
It comes with
No warrantee, replacement parts,
Or a 60-day return policy.

But it does come with instructions,
Couched in a secret place.
You can't read it with the naked eye.
The print is too fine.
If you take the time to look,
You will find it.
Pick up a magnifying glass.
Go ahead. Read.

"Important safety information concerning use.
This product is guaranteed not to last.
Use it wisely. Do not abuse it.
The manufacturer is not responsible
For any damages incurred to this article.
We strongly advise you to treat other articles
Akin to yours with the same attention
You give to your own.
Do not hurtle it at other products.
They will break. Yours will break.
The usefulness of our product
Depends on cooperating
With other products.
Treat it with care,
And it will serve you well."

It's all in the fine print.
Search for it. Read it. Act.
You will not be sorry.

The Late-Blooming Flower *and Other Poems*

Sickness is a garment
that doesn't become or fit;
too loose, too tight,
too short, too long,
it never is just right.

The fabric is so heavy
it weights the wearer down,
the color drab and listless,
a wan and dreary brown.

What tailor designed such clothing
with seams that zig and zag,
that the more we fidget and tug and pull,
it still looks like a rag?

The Late-Blooming Flower *and Other Poems*

Requiem

She says she's fine
It's expected
It's required
She says she's fine,
All the time.
With a smile on her face
And a limp in her gait
In the name of the game
She never complains.

Then one day she died,
Without a sigh,
And she never complained,
No, she never did complain,
'Cause it was the end,
The end of the game.

Everyone cried,
They all eulogized,
How she never breathed a word,
And her plight no-one heard.

But the pain she felt inside
She dared not confide,
Lest her debility disturb their tranquility,
Remind them of a day
When they could not pretend
Their play had no end.

(of her absence no-one speaks,
it's been but a week)

Suffering is deemed a virtue
by those acquainted least;
they say it builds one's character,
yet never go out of way to meet.

But once inside the edifice,
caught in a revolving door,
they seek to find an exit,
and not be built at all.

The Late-Blooming Flower *and Other Poems*

Variations on a Theme

Spoken with changing intensity and inflection on each repetition

Opus 1   Covid

Molto Adagio e espressivo

One

One

One

One

One

One

One

One

One

One

One

One

One

One

One

One

One
One
One
One
One
One
One
One
One
One
One
One
One
One
One

Uma

Ett

一つ

אֶחָד

One

Один

Uno

واحد

一

Mid

Vienas

एक

Kotahi

Մեկը

Hiji

Egy

1
1
1
1
1
1
1
1
1
1
1
1
1
1
1
1

2-1=1

3-2=1

4-3=1

5-4=1

6-5=1

7-6=1

8-7=1

9-8=1

10-9=1

11-10=1

12-11=1

13-12=1

14-13=1

15-14=1

16-15=1

17-16=1

One

SATU

I   (I)

Kotachi   I

①   -1x-1=

.1+.1+.1+.1+.1+.1+.1+.1+.1+.1=

1

N

E   0

1/1

January 1, 2020

$1 \div 1 = 1$

Tasi

otu

ஒன்று ....

ENO

◁1

❶

100,000 x 10 = 1,000,000

10,000 x 10 = 100,000

1,000 x 10 = 10,000

100 x 10 = 1,000

10 x 10 = 100

1 x 10 = 10

The Late-Blooming Flower *and Other Poems*

I   -   1   =   0

A muffled whisper

A heartbreaking sigh

An ear-piercing scream

A mournful cry

Each is the voice

Of one who died

Dedicated to all past, present, and future victims of Covid-19

And those touched by their lives.

Toss a pebble into a pond,

See the circles go round and round

December 4, 2020

Nuances on Loneliness

alone
winter chill
greets me

asking for company
a waiting
cup of tea

lonely
winter chill
hugs me

alone
a cup
of hot tea

alone
paring down to
the bare essentials

loneliness
neighbors peering out
their windows
in a rainstorm

a cold rainy day
my space heater beside me

alone
walking on a
crowded street

dementia
she plays tea party
with her best friend
from elementary school

surviving on
make-do meals
shut-in

grief
I forget to
take out the trash

death
staring at
an old diploma

mourning
photos spread
on the table

grieving
reading old letters

mourning
listening
to saved phone messages

mourning
loading the truck
for the Goodwill store

a peek outside
one leaf
on a tree

moving day
memories settle
in the dust

grief
getting used to
the past tense

a lone leaf
family's moved on

Mother's Day
the scent of yellow roses –
fading

Father's Day
avoiding
the greeting card aisle

sunrise
your wake-up call

The Late-Blooming Flower *and Other Poems*

Convalescence – A Prelude

Muted colors
Muted sounds
Fragile breeze
Fallen leaves

I walk alone
in a wilderness
of memories

Pictures, books, letters,
Two Steinway pianos
That once sang
Poems of music
Closed like black coffins
Carrying my heart

Now it is the little things,
The blades of grass singing
Their way through concrete
That bring me draughts of life

I admire their fearlessness,
Their delicate strength
Saluting the light. Filled with their resolve,
I tidy up a bit –
Still life, another blade of grass
Singing a triumphant note
In a melody

Looking outside,
I am astonished to see
New green leaves of Spring
Covering the branches which
Just yesterday had been bare

after surgery, February 27, 2016

The Late-Blooming Flower *and Other Poems*

Funny thing about stains.
And spills. And weeds.
They just appear.
As they say,
Out of nowhere.

It's not that
You planned them,
Like you would
Landscape a garden,
Planting one here,
Another there.

Or how in
Decorating your house,
You artfully
Attach each article
To its rightful place.

They just show up,
Unwanted, unwelcome,
Trespassers in a well-planned domicile.
You wipe them up,
You pull them up.
With a vengeance.

And just as you think
You can restore your Eden,
And like God,
After six days of labor,
Can rest on the Sabbath,
Another appears,
Then another.

An endless battle.
The wily creatures
Camouflage themselves
In a barrage of tricks,
Or else boldly present
In a rage of color,
Never apologizing
For their waywardness,
Or with contrite hearts
Promising to turn their lives around.

We sigh. We lament.
Our labor is in vain.
Slavishly we spare no pains
To erase their sins,
A weed called Impeccability
Planted in our minds,
Enslaved to a polestar
We cannot reach,
Blind to the imperfection
That is perfection.

The Late-Blooming Flower *and Other Poems*

There is something so disquieting
about a house that I just saw,
it speaks of being empty,
of a dweller withdrawn.

Its look is just too crystallized,
a rigidity forlorn,
as bone bleached in a desert
that company once adorned.

Uninviting is its starkness,
and though I cannot see inside,
there's a plainness of interior
where no embellishings reside.

A canvas scarce of color,
surrounded by a frame,
it asks for an owner
to make house a home again.

Brief
(haltingly)

22 years old
two toddlers
a girlfriend
former prisoner
turning his
life around
asthma attack
lungs collapsed
paramedics came
tried to
turn his
life around
dad devastated
don't understand
sister grieving
tears hugs
no words
to turn
his life
around to
bring him
back from
asthma attack
huddled together
to keep
the soul
warm on
sunny day
blue skies
no wind
God wanted
him I
guess says
dad how
could God
want to
take my
son away
on such
a beautiful
fall day
even the
leaves are
on reprieve

in memory of Anthony Jr., son of my neighbor Anthony

Immortality stands ready
to supersede at death;
we wait for him so patiently,
but want to shun the rest.

So why not fling the door aside
and invite him in, our guest;
he only asks your company,
so little, but not less!

The Late-Blooming Flower *and Other Poems*

The longest journey there must be
is from sickness to recovery,
when time is yawning wearily,
and sudden drifts to sleep.

Though cards are placed nearby like friends,
adorned with cheery flowers and birds,
well-wishing messages and inspirational words,
of time entreating to be speedily heard –
hasten the healing they do not,
but leave mending to wend its cryptic route.

Till seamlessly, the affliction departs,
as if it had never been;
Time resumes its steady course,
complaint erasing without remorse.

The Late-Blooming Flower *and Other Poems*

Drawn to eccentricity,
we abjure it all the same.
A proclivity to patterns
keeps us safe and sane.

What can I say to you, dear friend,
When the door is closing behind?
Words of hope?
Wishes for a speedy recovery?
Faith that a miracle will heal?
Comfort as your body wastes away?

No, all that is past.
Behind this litany of words, sifting like sand out of my fingers,
I cannot hide.
Pluralities that ride the tides of breath
Expire from where you, singular, rest.

Struck speechless, I grope for meaning,
And am answered by unspeakable silence,
Caught as a moth in the eye of a spinning vortex,
A flickering flame that sputtering, dies.

*Written without conscious knowledge,
within the two days my dear friend Sardar Singh passed away.*

Time embezzles Memory,
Robs it of its worth;
We beg for it, impoverished,
But are only left the dearth.

The Late-Blooming Flower *and Other Poems*

Do you have a secret drawer
closed discreetly with lock and key,
that no-one else is privy to,
and that you can scarcely see?

Is it strewn with things misshapen,
missteps that led astray,
or memories too sweet to bear
of loved ones gone away?

It's not so very strange, dear,
I have one just like you;
We share a sealed kinship
ensconced from public view.

The Late-Blooming Flower *and Other Poems*

Faith
will last
through
sunny
days

Too fast,
lightening
cannot wait
for correspondence
to take place

The Late-Blooming Flower *and Other Poems*

The Masters are oft quoted,
But I will listen to mine,
The spirit that dwells within me
Has a voice divine.

Someone's been sowing a secret
scattered in the sky,
that no-one can decipher
from birth until they die.

The closer one approaches,
the more recedes at bay,
as if modesty reproaches
and bows itself away.

The Late-Blooming Flower *and Other Poems*

Obituary

When I am gone,
and you are here,
remember that a
small bird tried
to sing, though its
voice was shattered
by the wind.

When I am gone,
and you are here,
remember that one
small bird tried
to fly, though it
flew with broken wings.

Then remember the
kind words it once said,
that laid wreathes of flowers
around your head.

Gather gently in your hands
that bird with broken wings,
that bird who tried to sing;
with its ashes scatter songs
of kindness to the winds,
that broken hearts may heal,
that broken wings may fly,
that one small bird
may never die.

The Late-Blooming Flower *and Other Poems*

"What is Life?",
asked the little girl
of her father.
"Ask the clouds",
he answered.
"What is Life?",
asked the girl
to the clouds.
And the clouds
replied with rain.

The little girl walked in the rain
until she came to the dry lake
which she had named Sandbox,
because she loved to bring her toys there and play.

But today, she could not play in her sandbox,
for before her stood a lake
filled to the brim with rainwater.
Suddenly the rain stopped.

"Where are my toys?"
she demanded of the lake.
"Look inside", answered the lake.
And looking down
into the calm, clear deep,
she saw her own reflection,
and was mute.

Dedicated to my friend Sardar Singh, whose insight "The purpose of Life is the expression of Itself", inspired this poem-story.

I am the river
Emptied into the sea
No longer the river
No longer me

The song I sing
Of sincerity rings
For that which is true
To the heart gives wings

Yesterday cannot contain my song
Nor tomorrow hold it
Your memory cannot capture it
For it is ever-present, always new
There is nothing it possesses
Nor does it seek to possess
It belongs to no race, nation, or creed
It is silence, shattering all barriers

You can hear it in the beating of your hearts,
In your smiles, in your tears
It is there in the first breath and the last,
In all your comings and goings
It is the song of a bird flying through
A clear blue sky – Where is its beginning?
Where its ending? Its melody is ever-changing
No tracks does it leave, no path can you follow

Then cherish my memory
But do not cling to it,
For I am not memory
My song is Life holding the hand of Death,
It is Love

In the silence of your listening
My song is with you
My heartfelt song is with you
But if you hear yourself alone,
Where is my song?
A bud opens, blossoms, dies, and falls.
Between Life and Death,
Is there a wall?

Listen to my song
It is a song for all

*Written in 1984 for the unveiling of the memorial plaque of
Bernard Shlutz, my father, who sang for all, and inscribed with the words
A Song for All*

The Late-Blooming Flower *and Other Poems*

Translation
(to be spoken out loud)

I am here

    (I am not leaving)

I am here

    (I am not fleeing)

I am here

    (I am with you)

I am here

    (I dedicate my life to you)

I am here

    (I dedicate my attention to you)

I am here

    (I dedicate my thoughts to you)

I am here

    (I dedicate my actions to you)

I am here

    (You are not alone)

I am here

    (My loyalty is with you)

I am here

    (I will never abandon you)

I am here

    (You are my family)

I am here

> (Together we defend our home)

I am here

> (Together we persevere)

I am here

> (Together we defend our freedom to be)

I am here

> (I am descended from David)

I am here

> (Together we will overcome Goliath)

I am here

> (I bear your sorrows)

I am here

> (My heart is with you)

I am here

> (I live for you)

I am here

> (I would die for you)

I am here

> (I love you)

Dedicated to Volodymyr Zelensky, President of Ukraine, who when offered help from the United States in leaving his country when it was invaded by Russia, responded with "I am here", three words which changed the world. Slava Ukraini!

March 16th, 2022

Index of Photos

Janine Cooper Ayres
Pages 32, 86, 100, 102, 106, 112, 116, 134, 210, 224, 322

csgee
Pages 30, 38, 74, 118, 122, 156, 166, 216, 244, 264, 284, 300, 318, 326

Donald H. Gudehus
Pages 20, 44, 66, 90, 98, 142, 154, 170, 176, 180, 238, 252, 254, 260, 288, 304, 312, 314, 316, 320, 324

D.V. Hardy
Pages 24, 48, 110, 202, 280, 334

JCMDI Digital Imaging, jcmdi.com
Pages 36, 92, 132, 146, 164, 206, 212, 214, 256, 258, 286, 308, 328

Miranda Knowles
Page 268

Kamy Merithew
Page 236

Bill Norton
Page 128

Frank M. Toothaker
Pages 5, 9 (David James original, photo on right), 16, 18, 22, 26, 28, 34, 40, 58, 62, 68, 80, 82, 88, 126, 136, 138, 150, 158, 160, 162, 168, 182, 186, 188, 192, 198, 222, 230, 266, 270, 272, 274, 290, 330, 332, 336, 338, back cover

Artists

Nancy Fierro
Page 96 – oil pastel

Diane Shields
Page 342 – Painting for Ukraine

Michael Vernetti
Page 52 – Mosaic, The Singing Village

www.ingramcontent.com/pod-product-compliance
Lightning Source LLC
Chambersburg PA
CBHW041202290426
44109CB00003B/104